Aural Sex
& Verbal Intercourse
Isadora Alman

DOWN THERE PRESS
Burlingame, California

Down There Press
P.O. Box 2086
Burlingame, California 94010

Alternative Cataloging in Publication Data

Alman, Isadora.
    Aural sex and verbal intercourse. Burlingame, CA: Down There Press, copyright 1984.

    First-person account of "working at San Francisco Sex Information," a telephone information-and-referral service. Characters are "invented composites" of real people.
    1. Sex information services—San Francisco—personal narratives.
2. San Francisco Sex Information—Personal narratives. I. Down There Press. II. Title: Oral sex and verbal intercourse. III. Title: Verbal intercourse and aural sex.

301.417 or 612.6

DEDICATION

To my SFSI family which may someday encompass thousands of people who find more joy than pain in sexual connections.

TABLE OF CONTENTS

In 1972 when Toni Ayres, Carolyn Smith and I started San Francisco Sex Information (SFSI) we wanted to provide up-to-date, non-judgmental sex information to San Francisco Bay Area communities. We didn't know how this would be received and hoped that SFSI would be useful and valuable for at least a few years. Now, twelve years later, SFSI has survived and grown. The hundreds of trained volunteers of diverse sexual orientations and lifestyles are a family for each other and have given support to thousands of all ages who call for information.

SFSI's community is nationwide—people call with all kinds of questions from everywhere. For many, SFSI is the first important contact in a process of growth towards acknowledging sexual feelings and behaviors as normal and natural. We have been raised in a high-tech sex-negative culture, woefully ignorant of our sexual rights. SFSI volunteers have committed themselves to thorough training and conscious responses to peoples' concerns. SFSI will continue to serve as a model of excellence to those interested in state-of-the-art sex education. My heartfelt thanks go to all the people who created and continue SFSI, and to the capable and dedicated Isadora Alman for telling the rest of the world about us.

Maggi Rubenstein, Ph.D., American College of Sexologists

A long time ago, a doctor wrote a book titled *Everything You Always Wanted To Know About Sex. . . But Were Afraid To Ask.* Frankly, I liked the movie better.

My problem with *Everthing* was that it was written as a definitive guide to sex and sexuality. While many of Dr. Reuben's "facts" were correct, more than just a few were judgmental and not supportive of individual sexuality and alternative lifestyles.

If Dr. Reuben accomplished anything with his book it was not the education of the public about sex. The reason his book was a landmark publication was because it was the first book about sex that became a best-seller. Its immense popularity opened the door for the likes of Shere Hite, Nancy Friday, and the G-Spot people.

Isadora Alman is not a doctor. Nor is she a chronicler of sexual trends or fantasies. She is a sexologist, counselor, and sex educator. Her interest in sex is not merely scholarly. She likes it. As a matter of fact, she enjoys it immensely.

It's this sex-positive quality that makes *Aural Sex and Verbal Intercourse* a very special book. Yes, it has sex information in it. Yes, the sex information is non-judgemental and supportive. But the book is a lot more than that.

Aural Sex and Verbal Intercourse is about communication. If the brain is the number one sex organ as some claim, then communication is the number one sex technique. The problem is that many people are uncomfortable talking about sex, even with their sex partner(s) — in some cases, *especially* with their sex partner(s).

Think of two people deciding to go to a restaurant. One loves spinach and scallops and sherbert and hates carrots and calf's liver and chocolate. The other loves broccoli and brisket of beef and blueberries and hates tomatoes and tamales and tapioca. Now picture these people trying to decide on a restaurant—without communicating their likes and dislikes. Not only will a decision be hard to reach, but the eventual dining experience will be less than exciting.

We all have our sexual menus. And we have to give ourselves permission to communicate our sexual likes and dislikes before, during, and after a sexual experience. *Aural Sex and Verbal Intercourse* is an important book because it encourages communication not only through what it says, but also by how it says it.

Staffing San Francisco Sex Information are ordinary people who have had an extraordinary experience: SFSI Training. One of the best sex education courses available, the Training is taught by people who not ony know what they're talking about, but live what they're talking about. We not only learn about sex, we learn how to share feelings and experiences with others, and most importantly, how to communicate what we learn and who we are to others. SFSI can change people's lives for the better. It sure changed mine.

Aural Sex and Verbal Intercourse is about people. It's about the people who have the questions and the people who have the answers. It's not written in a dry question-and-answer style; it reads like people talk. It talks in medical terms. It talks in street slang. It talks in hypothetical examples and in personal histories. But most of all, it talks *real*.

And while you learn about sex and sexuality, you also learn about the kind of people who volunteer to communicate the sex information. You learn to care not only about the callers, but about Sam and Pauli and the rest of the characters at the Switchboard. You experience a lot of what Isadora herself experienced. The time has come for a book about real people and real sexual concerns. *Aural Sex and Verbal Intercourse* is that book.

By the way, for information about SFSI Training, or for an answer to a sexually-related question, call the Switchboard at (415) 665-7300. Tell them Isadora sent you.

Tom Greensmith

Member, San Francisco Sex Information Board of Directors
Editor, S*I*N (Sex Information Newsletter)

THE TRAINING

The man to my left appeared to be sucking his own cock, but I couldn't be sure. To my right was a nude guy strapped to a table, who was being whipped lovingly by a redhead wearing a leather mask and metal brassiere. I considered momentarily what looked like a python swallowing a tree branch, but soon realized that it was a thin-faced woman kneeling before a swarthy porno film star more reknowned for his equipment than his acting talents. A few feet away was a hunky group of football players, some with and some without helmets and jock straps, huddled in a manner seldom seen on a playing field. Two buxom blondes were trying to arouse the interest of a very bored looking horse who in certain respects bore a startling resemblance to the porno star. Way over on the left, two women—one Asian, one black—were cavorting in a bath tub. On the edge of the tub was a cucumber and a bottle of Breck shampoo. I couldn't imagine what they might do with the shampoo that wouldn't sting.

I looked for a moment at a closeup of a woman's contorted face. Was she having her feet cut off? Something horrendous must be happening below my field of vision. When the camera pulled back I saw that she was in fact being attended to by a Germanic young man in the missionary position. Ho hum.

Below them was a series of slides from a Japanese erotic manual. All those bland faces and bulging blue-veined penises amid intricately folded robes; I had seen them before.

In the background, at almost deafening volume, a girlish voice with an English accent recited the balcony scene from *Romeo and Juliet*. My attention turned again to the man in the lower left corner. By god, he had at least two inches of his own cock in his mouth. If he did that often, no wonder he was roundshouldered.

"Goodnight, goodnight. Parting is such sweet sorrow
That I will say goodnight till it be morrow."

The lilting British voice was stilled. All the screens faded to black, willy nilly and coitus interruptus, and the lights came up on fifty sets of eyes blinking at the sudden brightness. It was Monday evening, halfway through the third session of the Sex Information Volunteer Training program. The 45 minute media blitz we had just witnessed was the infamous Fuckerama.

At the ten minute break, those of us with addictions and/or weak bladders crowded into the narrow hallway where the only ashtray and the washrooms were located. I lit a cigarette, leaned against the wall, and read the name tags pinned to my fellow trainees. We'd been instructed this evening to write our names and something sexual we hadn't tried and would like to. Hal wanted a threesome with two women. Gordon coveted his neighbor's wife in a hammock, Gilda dreamed of a ménàge à trois and Leanne yearned to do it hanging from a chandelier. I had a vision of Hal and Gilda joining forces looking for a fourth hand in some wild game of bridge.

So far, the course had been a mind boggle for me, the first April Training weekend was already a blur. We had covered the history of the Sex Information Switchboard, sex research through the ages, men's and women's sexual physiology and response, hetero-, homo- and bisexuality, our own sex histories related in small groups, and masturbation discussed with a member of the group chosen at random. I could see the value of the latter exercise to liven up dull cocktail parties. Oh yes, we covered oral sex that first weekend too. Chile, actually and legally Honey Chile Williams, one of the presenters of that lecture, called it "oral caress." I thought that sounded a great deal better than "blow jobs" and "eating out."

The break was over, new things in store. If the Training

Staff was going to play "Can You Top This?" after the Fuckerama, they were going to have a tough time of it.

In the presentation on anal sex that followed there was a film in which an anus of indeterminate gender (I'm sure it had a gender though I couldn't decipher it) accommodated a large man's finger, then fingers plural, then hand and wrist. I daydreamed about some sort of Olympic event, a name for which I couldn't imagine, in which the owner of the accommodating anus would be matched against the woman with the python-like jaw.

We dispersed into assigned small groups to discuss our reactions to the evening's topics. Individual responses to the sexual smorgasboard of the visual blitz were as varied as the acts we'd seen: boredom, anger, arousal, amusement, amazement, disgust, dismay, delight, and disbelief. I felt them all. I decided to take notes for myself on the rest of the Training.

Second Monday night: Write on your name tag something you haven't told your partner and would like to. Communication night. I could see its point after I'd spent the evening parading around with strangers reading and commenting upon a very simple directive I had been too embarrassed to tell the only one who needed to hear it, my regular sexual partner. Rob, a beautiful bearded young man of twenty-one read my tag and smiled, "You never told your lover you like that? I prefer it that way over almost everything else."

The following night, I recounted the whole evening's happenings to my honey. He got the message. Thank you, Switchboard Training.

Third Monday night: Potluck dinner at the home of one of the Training Staff. Good food, good conversation. . . about sex, of course. It's such fun for me to talk about what I imagine everyone is thinking about anyway—their own and other people's sex lives. What an incredibly diverse group of people are taking this class; all ages, colors, sizes and predilections. I wouldn't have expected to find much in common with Shirley, an intense college student of Chinese descent. However, we are both women—a bond of extreme intimacy and commonality once acknowledged. How important for me to rediscover that sense of. . . sisterhood. I don't remember feeling it with such intensity since my pregnancy almost fourteen years ago.

Second weekend: Saturday a casserole of sexual issues and ideas. Dolores, a well spoken Trainer in her late thirties, tells us of the endless rounds of psychiatric evaluations and pronouncements she endured in the 1960's in her efforts to have an orgasm in the "correct" way: through intercourse with a male partner, whom, of course, she must love enough to marry. I remember when I was doing it "wrong" too. Oh, the epithets: immature, frigid, unfeminine. I felt a surge of rage at the ignorance of the so-called helping professions. But then, barber surgeons used to bleed ailing people with leeches. They meant well too.

Long afternoon discussion on sexual lifestyles. What an array. Very Now Generation. Growing up, I knew of two choices only — married with children, or not yet so. Who knew such a buffet was available. Sounds wonderful!

Answering children's questions about sex. Non-consensual sex. Sexually-transmitted conditions. Sex and the disabled. Sex and aging.

Aging. My 39th birthday is less than a week away. A comic age, like a broken toe is a comic ailment, but painful nonetheless, at least for me. The woman in the film shown is mid-fifties, I'd guess. Her partner in sex, a bald, pot-bellied man with merry eyes and an engagingly wicked laugh. But this aging woman has the body of a young girl. (Better give it back before you get it all wrinkled. Ho ho.) Her breasts are small and perky, tummy flat, legs and ass well muscled and firm. This isn't aging as I see it and know it. Nothing sags, wobbles or billows. I never looked that good at eighteen. If this film is meant to be encouraging, it isn't working that way for me.

A practice phone call exercise with young Rob. He speaks of his fantasy of making love with an older woman. I try to remain a detached listener. I fail.

Sunday is an incredible banquet of esoterica — cross dressing, sex toys, body excretions as turn-ons. Sweat, okay, but feces? It gives a whole new meaning to the phrase "getting one's shit together."

To a hushed audience, Peter, one of the most attractive men on the Training staff, gives a lecture demonstration on S & M. In full motorcycle leathers, aviator glasses, and lots of "attitude" he struts his stuff. His lecture partner is a pudgy little woman in matching garb who looks even more macho than Peter. Macha? The weekend concludes on this awe-inspiring note. I am. . . boggled, "in overwhelm" as the Training Staff calls it. I'm not sure how I feel about all I've heard or what is relevant for me personally.

Fourth Monday night: Tonight's agenda is birth control, abortion, and giving birth. The abortion film, graphic and in color, occasions some bad memories and painful associations for several people. Another film, however, gets to me. Surrounded by friends and family in a wooded cabin, the midwife an intimate friend, a woman labors to give birth in an atmosphere of hushed celebration. I watch, enrapt, then realize with a jolt that I went to high school in New York with the woman giving birth. I am touched with wonder at witnessing again the miracle of birth, with nostalgia for the way things were not when my child was born. And with envy of my old schoolmate. Time nibbles at my ankles. Birthday blues. I surprise myself by dissolving into tears when the film ends, and find my solace, not in the tender concern of the Training staff, but in a time honored way. When the class is over I go home with young Rob.

Fifth Monday night: The last Switchboard Training Class. Help, I'm not ready. Do I know everything there is to know about sex? Okay, well then do I at least know how to find out? We cover ways to meet potential partners, touch on bestiality and necrophilia (if all other methods fail?) and gender issues with a transsexual guest speaker. In a flurry of shift scheduling, graduation party invitations, finishing business, and hugs from newly-made intimates, the Training is over.

Shirley and I exchange phone numbers. Rob and I share a moment of sweet smiling complicity as we hug goodbye. I approach Marla, the Training Coordinator, sure that she and I can become friends now that we are both members of the community, Switchboard volunteers.

1

WHO'S WHO

The tiny scrap of paper in my hand held the address of the Switchboard. I arrived there my first Thursday afternoon breathless and a few minutes late to see the comforting brush of Honey Chile's beard poking out of a car window. Handing me a rose, he wished me good luck on my first day. "Pauli and Sam are old pros, they're upstairs and will show you around. I'll be back before the end of your shift. Later." And he was gone.

In the main room of the small back apartment were four people. Two I recognized from the Training, two I did not. The strangers, no doubt Sam and Pauli, were seated at desks using the telephone. Pauli was speaking earnestly, the phone cradled between her neck and shoulder. With one hand she waved at me as I entered; with the other she was making circular movements in the air that the person on the other end of the phone couldn't possibly see.

"The clitoris sort of hides, see. It doesn't poke right out there like a man's sex organs. So what you have to do is rub in the general area where it was last seen before it went underground. If you make wide enough movements, you're bound to hit the right spot."

Sam, a 60ish man sporting a waxed moustache the likes of

which I'd never seen outside a barbershop quartet, sat leaning back with his feet on the desk. He was listening intently to the phone he was holding and did not look up.

I knew Stella, a frail-looking young women with a whispery voice, from a small group discussion in Training. She wore her coppery hair in two braids which reached to her waist. With her patchwork skirt and a crocheted shawl, my daughter would have dismissed her as a "hippie leftover." I was charmed by her aura of timeless feminine grace.

The other man I'd met in Training, but didn't know. He was a large man, tall and big, wearing cowboy boots and a cowboy hat, both black. He held out a mammoth hand and rumbled, "I'm James." I introduced myself. Stella murmured something, presumably her name, and smiled. We stood and looked around the cluttered room together.

The man with the moustache hung up the phone and rose to greet us, "I'm Sam." He shook hands with James, then laid a hand lightly on Stella's shoulder and on mine, a paternal gesture that I dislike. I stepped back and offered my hand. "How do you do, Sam. I'm Isadora."

Taking my outstretched hand, he enclosed it in both of his, effectively imprisoning mine. "The dancer?"

"No, I'm the *other* Isadora," my standard line with those who feel compelled to refer to Isadora Duncan.

Sam laughed and patted my shoulder again, sliding his hand down my arm until it came to rest at my elbow which he held as he guided me into a small room off the kitchen. He motioned with his chin for the other two to follow. "Let's go in here. Pauli will join us when she's off the phone. Chile was supposed to be here to show you around."

"He was here. He let me in." I held up my rose by way of explanation. Stella, I now noticed, wore one at the end of a braid. James had tucked his in the brim of his hat.

Hand still on my arm, Sam gestured expansively with the other. "Feel free to browse and poke about at your pleasure. You all know the basic drill. We'll be here Thursday afternoons from 3 until 6. Sign in when you come in to keep track of your volunteer commitment. There's a sign-in book somewhere in this clutter. We have a fully equipped kitchen, bring whatever you want for sustenance. There's always coffee and tea. No liquor or drugs here ever, you know that," Sam went on. "We keep log books by every phone. Try to list the caller's gender if you can deduce it, age if you can get it, his concern, and, if possible, where he heard about the Switchboard."

"Are most of the callers men?" Stella's soft whisper.

"Because I didn't use the politically correct 'his or her' name, age and gender?" Sam grinned.

"I was just wondering," Stella answered mildly.

Sam sat down and leaned back, a dangerous undertaking in the casterless swivel chair he occupied. "Actually, yes, I would say that the majority of our callers are men, or boys, males anyway. We get an overabundance of calls from male teenage jerk-offs. No offense, people. I know there are adult jerk-offs too. Some of my best friends, etcetera, and yea, even I. But to answer your question, little lady . . ."

Stella didn't wince. I did.

"Most of our callers are male," Sam continued. "Maybe women get their honest answers elsewhere, but I doubt it." He picked up a spiral notebook from a pile on the floor and read aloud:

Male, 12: What's an orgasm? Sperm?—Friend recommended us.

Male: How to on oral sex.

Male: Referral to urologist—Recommended by Gay Switchboard.

Female, 16: Being pushed by boyfriend to have intercourse. Her teacher told her about Switchboard.

Female: Where to meet Lesbians. Newspaper story.

Caller hung up.

Male, 15: Girlfriend may be pregnant. Heard from friend.

Male, 19: Penis size anxiety.

Male, 23: Wants safe positions for intercourse during wife's pregnancy. Recommended by her gynecologist.

"That will give you some idea," Sam concluded. "What I just read was one volunteer's report of one, albeit one very busy, shift. At least we don't lack for variety around here."

"Ta da!" sang out the tall woman swooping through the doorway. "Hello, everybody, I'm Pauli. Sorry I couldn't get off the phone sooner. I was teaching a bottom the art of negotiating an SM scene. How do you like 'pickle' for a safe word? Hello? Am I going too fast for you? I forgot, you're just out of

Training, still wet behind the ears – or better yet, between the legs."

Barely stopping for breath she smiled at Stella who was seated closest to the door. "Speaking of bottoms, Sam patted yours yet?" Without waiting for an answer she looked at me. "More likely yours, am I right?" Without pause Pauli went on. "What has Sam the Man been telling you? Complaining about our jerk-off callers, as he calls them? Hey, don't be fooled by his gruff act. His heart is almost as big as he claims his dick is. And don't let him bullshit you either. After all those years of teaching college kids he's a master of the art."

"Do sit down, Pauli." Sam pointed to a chair. "Have you taken the phones off the hook? I was just getting to the good part, the exercise of my prurient interest. What brought you to the Switchboard, James?"

"I get advanced credit by doing this."

"No prurient interest of your own? No social worker's instinct? What work do you do? Are you a student?"

James's chair creaked ominously as he shifted his bulk. His large hands were laced together on the crown of the black cowboy hat on his lap, almost obscuring it. "I'm a nurse."

I immediately thought of the old Mike Nichols and Elaine May routine. A young man is telling his breathlessly eager parents of his interest in medicine, of his willingness to undertake the long years of study ahead, of the prestige awaiting him at the end. "Just think how proud I'll be," sighs the mother with a Yiddish accent. "Yes," the young man concludes. "You'll be able to introduce me to all your friends as my son. . . the nurse."

Twenty years ago that was an uproariously funny punchline. When James said "I'm a nurse," even in his rumbling basso, it didn't strike me in any way remarkable.

"And you, Red?" Sam turned to Stella. "You're a Sumo wrestler, no doubt."

Stella blinked. "I have been accused of that. I do massage at a health club."

"Really?" Sam's mouth twitched, and with it his bizarre moustache. "You look like you have the strength of a kitten."

"I'm stronger than I look," Stella spoke up. "I'm also a student midwife. I know a great deal about human bodies, but there's always more to learn."

"And you?" Sam faced me.

"Aha! Now he pounces. Right, Sam the Man?" Pauli gloated. "I don't mean to embarrass you, what's your name? Isadora? But you're definitely Sam's type. Zaftig. Is that the word, Sam?"

I sighed.

"What does that mean?" asked Stella, who'd never had and never would have that word applied to her.

"Juicy, I think," rumbled James, surprising me

Sam laughed, "Well put. I would have said voluptuous, but I like your choice of word better. There are some who'd say *all* women are my type. Well, Isadorable, what are you doing here?"

"I wanted to do some volunteer work. And since I like sex, this kind of counseling really appeals to me. I can't wait to get on the phones."

"Now?" Pauli said with uncharacteristic brevity.

"Sure. Why not?"

"Good for you. A get-up-and-doer," Pauli beamed on us all. "Sam and I have very different styles on the phone. You'll develop you own. We'll both be standing by to answer whatever you can't handle. There's a large binder on each phone desk called The Quickie Book which isn't about two-minute fucks. It's an alphabetically-arranged synopsis of everything you learned in the Training, methods of birth control, symptoms of diseases, state sex laws, etcetera. There's an index full of referrals—therapists, clinics, good doctors, that sort of thing. I'm going to take a call first. Listen and learn. Then you can take it from there, okay?"

We trooped back into the main room. Sam put one phone back on its cradle and it rang immediately. Pauli cocked her finger like a starter's gun and spoke into the mouthpiece.

Painted Toes

Pauli: Sex Information. Can I help you?

Caller: Can I talk to someone?

P: You are. Talk away.

C: Well, I was just reading the newspaper and I saw this full page ad with the headline "Summer Is Here" and it was filled with pictures of sandals. You know, the latest footwear for summer. I thought to myself, "Hoo boy, here we go again. I'm in for several months of a constant hard-on."

P: You were turned on that much by a newspaper ad?

C: Not really the pictures in the paper. I do enjoy looking at women's fashion magazines, though, when the ads are in color. The thing is, I find painted toe nails on women very erotic. When women wear shoes with their toes sticking out, well, for me that's like they were walking around bare-assed—instant turn on.

P: Women's painted toe nails by themselves are a turn on for you, is that what you're saying?

C: Yeah. Isn't that weird?

P: Do you think it's weird?

C: Well, most pictures that are supposed to be exciting, like the girly mags, show tits and ass, even wide open genitals. . . Men poke each other and leer when a women in shorts or a low-cut blouse walks down the street. That's all fine. But if I see a woman whose toes are sticking out of her shoes, and they have polish on them, I don't care if she's young or old. It doesn't matter if *she's* sexy, her feet are sexy as hell to me. I mean, some men talk about a great pair of tits like they weren't attached to a person. Painted toes are like that for me. Why is that?

P: You want an instant answer?

C: Sure.

P: Sorry, I don't have one. Let me ask you something: do you like asparagus?

C: Huh? No, not particularly.

P: Does that bother you? Would you be willing to go into therapy to find out why you don't, or into behavior modification to get you to like it more?

C: No. But painted toes aren't like asparagus.

P: You're right. They're more like lollipops, aren't they? Did you like lollipops a lot when you were a kid?

C: (Laughter) Not particularly.

P: Oh well, one instant analysis just shot to hell. But my point is, asparagus or painted toes, it isn't a problem unless it *is* a problem. Do you get me?

C: Yes, but. . . I grew up as a normal American boy. I like girls. I used to take a peek in class when some girl bent over and showed her panties, but I was really hoping she'd take her shoes and socks off. I look at Playboy's centerfold. I mean, the monthly lovely is holding onto her breasts and everybody's panting, but she's sitting on her feet and I can't see if she has polish on her toes. My favorite part wasn't even considered important enough to photograph! Why am I so different from all my fellow girl watchers?

P: Back to asparagus again. You know, some people really love the stuff and will pay five dollars a pound to have some in December. Do you think *they* think they're weird?

C: I think they are!

P: Well, there you jolly well are. You know that old saying: One man's meat is another man's poison. The whys and wherefores of anyone's tastes—in food and in sex in particular, are shaped not only by culture, but by all sorts of individual happenings in the past. Maybe the first time you were aware of an erection, you were a crawling infant with a view of the world restricted to feet. "I feel good feelings down there; I see a woman's painted toe nails." Bingo, instant erotic connection. Why do some men turn on to fat women in spite of our society's obsession with slenderness? These things are not conscious choices. You can be glad that your particular preference isn't hideously embarrassing or likely to get you into trouble with the law. Some people can only get turned on if they are making it in Macy's window wearing diapers. Does your turn-on cause any major problems for you?

C: No, not really.

P: Are you getting enough of painted toes in your life?

C: Never enough!

P: You didn't say, do you have a regular partner?

C: Nobody special. I date several women. I'm always looking.

P: Do the women you date paint their toes?

C: Some of them do. Some I don't even know if they do. I haven't gotten that far, or they don't wear the right kind of shoes.

P: So that isn't the only thing that attracts you to a woman?

C: No, of course not. Personality, compatibility, that kind of thing is extremely important if I'm going to spend any time with someone.

P: Would it be possible for you to ask to see the feet of a woman you're dating, offer a foot massage, or just plain out tell her that you like open-toed shoes and painted nails?

C: Wouldn't she think I'm awfully strange?

P: She might. And she might do it anyway if she knows it would please you. When you're together you could point out the types of shoes you like and say, "I find shoes like that sexy," or "Do you paint your toe nails?" I really am attracted to women who do."

C: But she might think that's so peculiar.

P: She might. She might think so too if you refused to share the asparagus she ordered for dinner.

C: Here we go with that asparagus again.

P: But you liking painted toe nails may not seem any more remarkable to a person than you not liking a certain vegetable. She might share your preference or she might not. She'll think you're weird, or she won't. You don't have to be more embarrassed about one than the other. Have you ever painted a woman's toenails for her?

C: Oh, I'd love to do that!

P: Well, how likely are you to get a chance to unless you offer? How about painting your own?

C: What?

P: I don't mean you have to go public. An investment of about two dollars will get you a bottle of polish and a bottle of remover. You can play all by yourself in private, and you can even have the pleasure of choosing the absolute most turn-on shade of red.

C: (Laughing) That sounds like masturbating.

P: Do you do that?

C: Sometimes.

P: Well then, this can be your own special variation. If liking painted toe nails is your own thing, you might as well go for it—however and wherever.

C: Hey, I've enjoyed talking with you.

P: My pleasure.

C: Can I ask you one more question?

P: Shoot.

C: Do you paint your toe nails?

P: Well, now that I know that there are connoisseurs like you out there, maybe I'll start.

C: Great. Keep our country beautiful. Thanks again.

"That was really creative, Pauli, right up your alley," Sam was laughing.

"I could only hear your end of the conversation," James said. "I'm not sure what his problem was."

"He didn't have a problem." Pauli waved her hands in the air and shrugged. "He only thought he did."

"Many people call for permission," Sam spoke. "Is it all right to do what I do, feel what I feel? All right with *me*? I don't care what anyone does as long as they don't do it in the street and scare the horses. I forget who said that originally, but it still serves, horses or no. What these callers are looking for is reassurance, validation."

"I think I've been in California too long," I said. "Whenever I hear someone in a restaurant hand his parking stub to the hostess and ask to be validated, I always expect her to look deep into his eyes and state, 'You're a fine human being.' "

Sam smiled. "But you will notice that in some form or another, that will really comprise a very large portion of our calls: Am I normal? And you will say. . . ?" I could just see the college teacher in Sam needing classroom participation.

"If whatever you do is consensual, legal, and doesn't scare the horses," James sing-songed.

"And if it's all right with the caller himself. . . or herself." Sam glanced at Stella wryly.

The phone rang again. "You're on, Isadora," Pauli pointed at me. With an almost steady hand I reached over to take my first Switchboard phone call.

On Becoming A Woman

Isadora: Sex Information. May I help you?

Caller: Does it hurt when you get your period?

I: Does it hurt? It doesn't have to.

C: Yeah, but does it sometimes?

I: Some people have cramps in their bellies, some have aches in the lower back. Some women feel as if they have to pee a lot and that can be a nuisance. It's different for different women, and it changes from time to time for each of us. Does the idea of having a period scare you?

C: My mom calls it "being unwell" and she goes and lies down in her room. My brother and I have to be real quiet and get our own dinner. But my PE teacher says that if you don't get dressed for gym, you're babying yourself. She says that menstruating is a perfectly natural function and we should just ignore it and let it take care of itself. How can you just ignore bleeding?

I: I can see why you're confused. Have you had any periods yet?

C: I did once, about two months ago. I haven't had another one since, so I'm not sure if I really started yet. Doesn't it come every 28 days?

I: Not necessarily every 28 days, especially at first, but most women eventually fall into some sort of regular pattern. It could be every 25 days, or 30 days, or somewhere in between. Lots of young women have a first period and then no more for a while, like you. Your body is simply working out the kinks, sort of getting the process working. What was your first period like?

C: Well, I felt sort of funny, like I was getting the flu or something, kind of achey. When I went to the school bathroom there was blood on my panties. I almost fainted. There's a tampax machine in the girls' room but I don't know how to use them, so I just stuffed some toilet paper between my legs and went home. When I told my mom, she told me to go to my room and lie down. Later she brought me a box of napkins that stick to your panties.

I: Did she say anything else about it?

C: No. But she said I didn't have to wash the dinner dishes and that she'd write me an excuse from gym class for the next few days.

I: It sounds like your mother feels that women really are sick when they are menstruating. Did you feel well enough to wash the dishes or to take gym?

C: I didn't feel sick, just funny. When I gave my PE teacher the note from my mother she gave me that lecture about women's normal body functions, and she acted annoyed.

I: It certainly seems your mother and your teacher experience their periods differently. No two women are exactly the same.

It's *your* body and your feelings; only you can tell what's going on with you. Women athletes and women politicians don't disappear several days each month. We have no way of knowing if they're feeling perfectly fine or not. They just go about their business as best they can. When you get your next period, and I'm sure you will soon, see how you feel. I can understand that it might be nice to get out of doing the dishes if you can, or cut gym class if you don't like it. But if you act as if you're unwell, you might get to feel unwell, and that's no fun.

C: Yeah.

I: Be sure to eat correctly, get some exercise. If you do get cramps or aches, an aspirin, a warm bath, resting with a heating pad, might be all you need to carry on normally.

C: Can I ask you. . . ? Do you get cramps bad?

I: Once in a while. I crawl in bed early with a good book. If I'm busy, or there's something I really want to do, I just try to ignore it. I think a monthly inconvenience is a small price to pay for the pleasure of having a child. I have a daughter about your age, and I'm very glad to be a mother.

C: I don't ever want to have a kid. I think this whole period business is a royal pain.

I: You might change your mind about having a child some day.

C: I really think it's unfair that guys don't have to go through this stuff. It's so embarrassing if you spot your skirt or something, and they can just laugh.

I: Oh, guys have their own problems. Boys' voices change as part of their growing up process. When their voice cracks in the middle of a class they get embarrassed too. Or what about an unexpected erection? Did you ever see a boy suddenly get red in the face and hold his books against his lap? That's a real problem for a lot of young men. I don't think I'd want to change places and be a teenage boy.

C: (Giggling) Maybe you're right. Getting a hard-on in class would be gross.

I: Do you want to talk about using tampons?

C: Not now. Maybe I'll call you back when I get my period again.

I: I hope you do. 'Bye now.

"To the manor born," Sam said when I hung up the phone. "You handled that as if you've been doing it all your life."

"But that's so real for me. I could have had that very same conversation with my daughter, and I probably have."

"Even after three wives and four daughters I'm never sure that I can say anything meaningful in that situation," Sam admitted. "All I can do is be sympathetic and mumble about 'woman's lot'. I am sympathetic, but when it comes down to it, I think a call of that nature is best handled by a woman."

"Like me." I suddenly realized, "What if I wanted her to call me back. How do I do that?"

"Use a phone-y name," Pauli answered. "Tell her your name is Bubbles La Rue or whatever, and that you're here every Thursday afternoon. I love to get follow-ups too, but I'm not always here."

"How come?" Stella asked.

"I met my time commitment more than a year ago but I know that afternoons are short-staffed, so I come in when I can. Anyway, whatever name you choose, be sure to write it on the volunteer board so people can refer your calls."

"Since Stella means Star, that's what I want to be called," Stella piped up.

"Stella, Star, do you want to take the next call?" Pauli asked.

"Not just yet, I think. I'd like to listen in on a few more."

The phone rang again. "I'll take it," James said, and he did.

Girl Talk

James: Sex Information. May I help you?

Caller: Oh. Uh, can I speak to a girl?

J: Just a minute please.

James covered the mouthpiece with his hand. "This caller wants to speak to a girl. What do I do?"

"It's a man asking, right?" Sam sighed.

"No," James shook his head. "It sounds like a young woman."

"I'm sure as shit no girl," Pauli said. "Stella, you come as close as we've got. Are you willing to take it?"

Stella shook back her braids, squared her shoulders, and motioned James to allow her to take over the desk.

Stella: This is Star. Can I help you?

Caller: Can you tell me, do girls look at guys?

S: Do they *look* at guys?

C: You know, *that* way, the way construction workers sit around on the sidewalk munching their lunch and making comments.

S: But there aren't that many women working in construction jobs. Is that what you mean?

C: No. See. . . um. I really dig guys' asses in tight jeans. I always check out a guy's buns. But I never heard any other girls say that they look, you know?

S: They do. I sure do. I like guys' asses myself. I just don't think that women are going to be that crass about it, the way some guys are. Wait, women can be crass too. I went to one of those male strip shows once? The women there were pretty rowdy in their admiration of the guys' bodies. It was fun. There wouldn't be these shows for women if they didn't pay to go. So I guess there are a lot of women interested in looking over guys' asses and other parts. Did I answer your question?

C: Yes. thanks.

S: Can I ask you how old you are? Hello?

Stella put down the phone and turned to us. "She hung

up before I could get her age or where she heard about the Switchboard."

"So you're an ass-watcher, hmm? Who would have guessed," Sam smiled.

"That's just fine, Star," Pauli broke in. "Sam is just teasing. You spoke from your own experience, which is exactly the right thing to do. James, thanks for checking about someone wanting to speak to a girl, although Lord knows, none of us is that. We do, unfortunately, get calls from men who get their jollies from talking to a woman about sex. They'll ask any question that comes to mind just so they can hear *those* words coming from a woman's mouth. Or better yet, they'll ask you to describe something in detail, like exactly how do women masturbate. You're halfway through your song and dance when you hear him beating out his own rhythmic accompaniment."

"We were told about that in Training," James said. "What would you prefer me to do in a case like that? Are you willing to have the call handed to you if a man asks? If I were a woman, I wouldn't. I'd feel abused and ripped-off."

"You might just tell a man who asked to speak to a woman that we've all received the same training and that you're sure you can answer his question," Sam instructed. "You could tell him there are no women free to take his call at that moment, but if the jerk-off is really determined, he'll just keep calling back and hanging up until a woman answers."

Chile had walked in unnoticed during our discussion. "You can always use Howard's method," he laughed. "He asks in a conversational tone: 'You want to speak to a woman? Oh, do you want to masturbate?' Then, if the guy says yes. . ."

"He tells him to stick it in his ear, right?" Pauli interrupted.

"Wrong." Chile went on, "If the guy says yes he wants to masturbate, Howard says in the same even tone of voice: 'I'm sorry, that's not what our service is for. Would you like to discuss some other ways you can get sexual satisfaction?' And then he'll talk about the pay services or about asking a friend to listen to you, stuff like that. He just turns it into a regular call. He doesn't make the guy feel bad though."

Sam shook his head. "Howard is more patient than I am."

"What if the caller denies he wants to masturbate over the phone?" James asked. "Suppose he says he would just feel more comfortable talking with a woman about personal things. I know some of the patients I take care of won't let me do certain things for them. They'll ask for a female nurse instead."

"Well, man, all you can do then is punt," Chile shrugged. "Spreading all this sunshine like we do, sometimes we get burned. If any of you feel like you're being ripped-off in any particular conversation, transfer it to someone else who's willing to tackle it or end the conversation. You guys are all we've got. If the volunteers burn out or turn sour we have no service, so take care of yourselves. How did it go today—any problems?" The question was addressed to all of us. His eyes, however, were on Stella.

"I enjoyed it," I said.

"Fascinating." James nodded.

Stella gave Chile a brilliant smile, "It's been great, so far."

"I hate to be the one to tell you this, kiddo," Pauli drawled, "but that's probably beginner's luck."

SETTLING IN

Only Sam was there when I arrived the following week. He looked up from turning off the phone-answering machine as I came in.

"Hello, Isadora. Stella called to say she can't make it in today. Schools are letting out this week, so be prepared for an onslaught of kid calls. Time on their hands and guess what the little buggers turn their minds to. Lord, whatever happened to baseball as the national sport? How are you this week, by the way?"

"Fine, Sam. Looking forward to being on the phones."

"Isadora, would you. . . ," Sam was interrupted in whatever he was going to ask by James's arrival. James carried a large bakery box. Lifting the cover for us, he diffidently displayed a chocolate cake, on the top of which, drawn in green icing, was a telephone receiver. Coming out of it were the words "Balls", "V.D.", "Suck" and "Fuck" in pink script. Sam whooped with laughter.

"Where in the world did you find a bakery to make that?" I gasped.

James chuckled at the thought. "I baked it myself. When

I worked in the kitchen at nursing school I never got a chance to be quite this creative. The vascular structure of an arm in red on white was the farthest I could go."

"It's magnificent, James," I gushed. "You're a man of multiple surprises."

"You ain't seen nothing yet, ma'am," he smiled. "Are there just the three of us today?"

"Looks like," Sam answered and set the log book on his desk. The phone rang and he picked it up where he stood.

The Tit Fancier

Sam: Sex Information. . .

Caller: Can you. . . tell me why women wear bras?

S: Why they wear bras? To hold their breasts, keep them from wobbling.

C: Why do they wobble?

S: Why? Breasts are fatty tissue. Depending on how big they are there is more or less to move around. And as a woman gets older they may get less firm and need the support of a bra. Not all women wear them. It's a matter of fashion and comfort.

C: How do tits. . . uh, breasts feel?

S: To have them? I don't know, I'm a man too. Or do you mean to the touch?

C: Yes. How do they feel to touch?

S: Like what they are, part of a human body.

C: Can you bite them?

S: I'd strongly suggest you get permission from their owner first. Look, guy, what's with this breast biting bit? I realize that breasts give you a big charge. I agree with you, they are things of beauty and a joy to behold, but they are part of a woman's body. And if you're ever going to find out what they look like, feel like, smell like, etcetera, you're going to have to quit jacking around on the phone to us and get out there and meet some women. Maybe then you can find out for yourself.

James and I both stared in amazement as Sam banged down the phone. What was that about?

"That's hardly what I'd call non-judgmental and supportive," James said evenly, "Wasn't that a kid?"

"It was not!" Sam shook his head in exasperation. "That guy calls at least twice a week. Look." He strode into the office and came back with a notebook labeled 'Chronic Callers.' "You can read all about him in here. His history dates back almost eight months. There's got to be a better system than this to alert the new volunteers. If either of you had taken that call you'd still be on the phone assuring our guy that yes, with permission, breasts can be bitten. They can be poked, pushed, prodded, tickled, twiddled, and tweaked until he'd exhausted his repertoire of provocative verbs. He would be no wiser for all your efforts. Look through this book. You'll get to know all the chronics sooner or later. I know I sounded far from sympathetic, but listen, I've answered his litany at least five times myself. He won't admit his real fears, and I'm tired of his wasting our valuable time when there are people we could be talking to who might benefit from our wisdom. You're welcome to handle it differently when he calls again, and he will, I assure you. Just be careful you don't re-invent the wheel."

He stalked into the bathroom and slammed the door. We stood there in embarrassed silence with the imaginative cake on the desk between us.

James brought three plates and a knife from the kitchen and began to slice it. I was sorry there weren't more people to appreciate his creation, or photographs to immortalize it. I wished for Pauli's applause, for Stella's girlish glee. When the phone rang again my mouth was full of one of the frosting "uck"s so James took the call.

What's Left To Do

James: Sex Information. May I help you?

Caller: Probably not, but what the hell.

J: I'm willing to try if you're willing to talk.

C: Talk, talk. Is that what they mean by oral sex? Ha ha. That's a joke, mister.

J: I'm listening.

C: Are you good at that? Do you get off that way?

J: Does it turn me on listening to people's sexual questions? I don't think so. I try to be a good listener. I'm willing to listen to you if you want to talk about something specific.

C: I don't want to talk, I want to fuck.

J: I can't help you there.

C: Nobody can. I'm paralyzed, a quadraplegic.

J: Ah. . . I see.

C: That's it? Just "Ah, I see." No "Awwww?" No "Gee, I'm sorry?"

J: You didn't call for sympathy, did you?

C: I don't know why I called. I got this new phone that I can operate with a special do-hicky courtesy of Ma Bell. It came with a directory of service organizations. Sex Information sounded interesting, so I called you. What the hell. So, what can you do for me?

J: I don't know. Do you have a sexual partner?

C: Yeah, my wheelchair, but I don't know whether it's a girl or a boy.

J: Is there someone in your life you can have sex with?

C: Man, I can't *have* sex anymore! I'm paralyzed from my shoulders down. I can't even pull my own pud.

J: You said it yourself, there's oral sex.

C: I can't feel anything down there.

J: Where do you have sensation?

C: Only from my shoulders up.

J: Well your mouth works just fine. You could give head to someone else, enjoy your partner's pleasure. You can discover things to do that feel good where you can feel it.

C: I never heard of anybody having sex with their neck.

J: You never heard of necking? Or mind fucking? Er, that's a joke.

C: Very funny.

J: Hey, I'm not making light of your situation, believe me, buddy. But sex doesn't have to equal a hard penis. It's about giving and receiving pleasure. You use what you've got. You have your mind, your imagination, your speech and some feeling and movement in part of your body. There can be pleasure in finding out what you can do, and can feel. . . think of it as being a kind of a virgin.

C: Look, mister. . .

J: My name is James.

C: Yeah, James. I can't talk any more right now. I'll call you back.

J: I really wish you would. I'm here until six every Thursday.

James hung up the phone and sat staring at the receiver.
"James?" I pulled over a chair to sit beside him. Sam touched his shoulder. "That's a hell of a first call for the day," I said. "It must have been very rough for you."
He looked up gravely. "Yes, it was. More so for the guy who called, I'd guess. I wonder why he hung up."
"I'm sure it was nothing you said wrong, James. That was a tough call. We can't know. Maybe someone else came into the room. Maybe he heard all he could handle for the moment. He might call back." Sam spoke with what I felt was rare gentleness. With a final pat to James's shoulder he went back to his desk.
I sat next to James, offering what comfort I could by my presence, each of us thinking our own thoughts in silence, until the next ring of the phone. It was not yet 4 o'clock, but I felt tired.

Coming Through The Rye

Isadora: Sex Information. May I help you?

Caller: I have this problem.

I: Yes?

C: Is there something I can do to last longer?

I: You want your erection to last longer?

C: Yeah. I come too soon.

I: Who says it's too soon? Do you come too soon as far as *you* are concerned, or is it your partner that says so?

C: Both of us, I guess. The last time I went to bed with this woman she said, "Is that it?" That must mean it was over too soon for her, right?

I: Can you tell me about it, what you did in bed?

C: What we did? The regular things.

I: Can you be more specific?

C: We kissed, undressed, I touched her breasts some. Then I reached down to see if she was. . . you know, ready. Then I got on top of her, put it in, moved my. . . cock in and out. . .

I: How long did you do that, would you say?

C: I don't know, maybe four or five minutes. Then I came.

I: Then what happened?

C: Then what? Nothing. It was over. I was going to say something nice to her like, "That was really great," before I got up and got dressed. But she hit me with, "Is that it?" and I felt like a fool. I gave her what I had.

I: Is that a typical sexual encounter for you?

C: I'm not sure what you mean. I was married for twenty years. We've been separated for the last few months. I've been to bed with maybe three or four women in that time. This last one I'm talking about, I thought I might get something going with her. I'd like to. But, hell, it's like she's saying I'm not much of a man. My wife never complained.

I: Was your wife orgasmic? Did she come when you had sex?

C: I don't know. Like I said, she never complained.

I: Sometimes a woman thinks it will hurt a man's pride if she makes a suggestion to do something different. Or she may not know there is anything different to do. Let's take this one point at a time. Yes, there are some things you can do to have your erection last longer. But first, you said your intercourse lasted four or five minutes, correct?

C: I never actually timed it.

I: The average length of intercourse is less than two minutes.

C: Oh yeah?

I: That's intercourse. In and out stuff with a hard penis, not sex in general. There is a difference. How long intercourse lasts can vary with your mood, with your partner, your age, whether you're tired or relaxed, whether you've been drinking. . . lots of things.

C: I have noticed that if I've had a few drinks, it takes longer for me to come.

I: That's your individual pattern. Many men come even more quickly if they've been drinking, or they have trouble getting an erection at all. It sounds like you are aware of your body and what works for you.

C: Hell, I should know. I've lived in this body for 43 years.

I: But you were having sex with your wife for 20 years and yet you don't know if she had orgasms or not.

C: But . . . .

I: I'm sorry. That's irrelevant. You know that old expression, "Different strokes for different folks?" It's literally true for sex. What you did with your wife might have been just fine with her. You didn't mention your having any problem about coming too soon when you were married.

C: I didn't think I had a problem then.

I: You may not have. That's why I asked whether "too soon" was too soon for you or too soon for your partner. With this particular woman you *may* have a problem. You seem to be assuming that if the intercourse had lasted, let's say, eight minutes instead of four or five, she would have been satisfied.

C: Isn't that right?

I: Not necessarily. This woman might have wanted more affection, more conversation before or during, more clitoral stimulation, more playfulness, different positions—any number of things.

C: I don't know her that well.

I: Let's suppose, though, that what she did want was more intercourse. What could you do about that?

C: I don't know. That's what I'm asking you.

I: Okay, here's one possibility. What might happen if after you came, instead of getting up and getting dressed, you stayed there in bed and continued to touch each other?

C: That's not intercourse. Besides, I don't like my cock touched after I come. It hurts.

I: She doesn't have to touch your cock. You might just snuggle together.

C: What does that have to do with anything?

I: I'm getting to that. You said you might want to get something going with this woman. Wouldn't this be a good time to lie together and talk? You might stroke or pet her casually, not necessarily sexually. You might share some of your sexual fantasies, or tell her what you like about the way she makes love with you. If you keep the connection going by talking and touching, you just might get another erection fairly soon, and have another go at intercourse.

C: Hey, I'm 43, not 23.

I: Two erections within an hour, let's say, may not have been your pattern even when you were 23, but who knows. This is a new woman, a new time in your life. It's worth a try. You might surprise yourself. If you get another erection, it will probably last longer just because the edge of eagerness has worn off. Here's another thing to try. When you first get into bed together and you're aroused, you could decide not to enter her right away.

C: Why else would we be in the sack?

I: I mean you can do other sexual things, come, continue to be together. Then, when you're hard again, you can enter her. It will probably last longer that time, and she may be more aroused and eager. Some men even masturbate early in an evening when they expect to have sexual intercourse later. Since they've come once that evening, when they're with a partner it's not such a pressing need, so they can take their time.

C: I don't know if I can do that.

I: Another thing you can do to last longer is to stop from time to time in the middle of intercourse.

C: Just stop?

I: Yes. When you've entered your partner, at first just stay there. Then move a little, slow down, stop, change positions maybe. All of these little interruptions give you a chance to catch your breath. The level of your excitement recedes some so that you can gather up steam again.

C: Oh yeah?

I: Some men hope it will help them to lower the level of excitement to think of other, non-sexual, things while they're having intercourse—like reciting multiplication tables or base-ball lineups. Have you tried that?

C: Yeah.

I: Doesn't work does it?

C: Didn't for me.

I: It seems a pity to me to tune out the pleasures of the moment just to be some ideal of a super stud. You can get the same effect by varying what you do and paying attention to it as well, changing to positions that feel good but aren't giving you exactly the right friction to trigger orgasm. It's helpful to tell her what's going on too. Like, "Let's stop a minute. I find you so exciting and I don't want to come just yet."

C: Yeah, I guess.

I: Most women will be pleased that you're enjoying them and thinking of ways to prolong the pleasure for both of you. These changes in speed, activity, positions, are all ways to last longer. The actual clocked time of in-and-out intercourse may still not be more than your average, but it will feel like it is. Or, in fact, it may prolong the actual time of intercourse—two minutes at this, one minute at that. It adds up.

C: I don't know whether I can do that. I'm no athlete.

I: How long has it been since you had a bathroom accident?

C: You mean wetting my pants? Not since I was a kid. Why?

I: Very early in life you learned to hold it in until you could get to a bathroom. Everyone does eventually. If you could learn to control those muscles as early as two or three years of age, it's certainly possible to learn to control those same muscles for sexual pleasure now.

C: Oh yeah.

I: There is the Eight Step Technique which is exactly that—a series of eight exercises in control. The exact instructions are in an excellent paperback called *Male Sexuality.* Briefly outlined, a man first masturbates alone, and when he feels he is nearing an orgasm, simply stops what he's doing until the feeling passes. After practicing alone and learning to recognize that instant before it's too late to stop, he goes on to do the same thing with a partner stroking him, stopping when he indicates, and then continuing. This method takes time, practice, and a co-operative partner, but eventually it does work.

C: You gave me a few ideas. Are there any more? I might as well hear whatever you've got.

I: Okay. Since it works for you already, have a drink or two before sex. You didn't mention what you do about birth control, but wearing a condom, especially one of the thicker brands, can decrease sensitivity and maybe prolong an erection.

C: The drink sounds okay. Scratch the rubber. What do you think I should do?

I: What do I think? I think you should set your priorities. If what you want is to have orgasms from sex with a woman, you have no problem at all; you're already doing that. If what you want is to keep your erection longer before ejaculation, besides some of the exercises and practices I mentioned, age is on your side. Most men, as they grow older, need far more stimulation in order to reach an erection and climax. So in another few years the problem may take care of itself. But if what you want is to satisfy this partner or any others, you need to find out more about women's bodies in general, and your partner's body in particular.

C: How do I do that?

I: There is no secret password: "This is what women like; do that and you'll be a good lover." Most women like clitoral stimulation. A tentative finger inside her vagina to see if she's wet won't do it. You can stimulate her vagina and clitoris before, during, or after intercourse. . . or instead of it. If she has an orgasm, or more than one, while you're doing that, then maybe you won't feel pressured to last any longer during intercourse than you do now. By the way, do you know where and what the clitoris is?

C: Yeah. It's that little bump.

I: Right. Okay, besides some stimulation that's not intercourse, this woman might want gentle handling, or a rougher touch than your wife did. Learn to read body language, to ask. The next time a woman says to you, "Is that all?" you can show her with your hands, your penis, your whole body—with or without an erection—that there's a lot more where that came from.

C: Yeah. Thanks a lot.

"You sounded like Pauli," James said to me when I finished that call, meaning it as a compliment, I hoped.

"Was I too flip?" I fretted. "Somehow I couldn't be overly sympathetic. I'm relieved it didn't show. I kept thinking about your caller, James, and what he wouldn't give for just thirty seconds of intercourse. And this guy sounded so unconscious — roll on, stick it in, roll off."

"Touched a nerve, did it?" Sam prodded.

"I don't know. Maybe. I've never been rude enough to say, "Is that all?" to a man, but there are sure times that I thought it. Maybe he and that woman deserve each other! Did you listen to any of it, Sam? Did I sound unsympathetic?"

"You covered everything very well," he assured me. "It's a very common call, you know. Everyone is convinced that everyone else does it better and has better equipment with which to do it; men *and* women, but especially men. You said everything that could be said — more than we often get a chance to. Some callers speak to us on some level that calls forth instant empathy. You handled that young girl's first menstruation that way. Other callers hit a nerve and it's hard even to be civil. Witness my blow-up at the tit fancier."

"Do you think men are better equipped — no puns now Sam — to handle men's concerns, and women, women's?" James asked.

"Sometimes," Sam said. "But all of us can define twat or finger-fucking with equal brevity, or make a referral, or explain a 'how-to'. If you really feel inadequate about answering a particular call, or it disturbs you to such an extent that you absolutely cannot remain non-judgmental, excuse yourself and pass along the call, just as Chile says. Don't worry about short-changing that caller. Yes, someone else might have handled that same call differently, even better, but if the caller feels he needs more, he can call back. Many of them do anyway, just to see if they can get an answer that they like better."

"Sure," James agreed. "Just because *you* say there is no secret password to being a good lover, Isadora, doesn't mean that *I* don't know one."

"James?" I couldn't resist. "Do you?"

"I am a man of many surprises," James quoted my own words back to me, and with a small smile turned away to answer the phone.

"Gooood line," Sam shook his head. "Would you like to hear some of mine, Isadora? Would you care to see my etchings?"

"Is that one of your lines, Sam? Tsk tsk. I do thank you, but no I wouldn't."

"Well, damn." Sam looked mock-perplexed. "I thought since you're a Switchboard volunteer, a supporter of healthy sex lives for all, you'd be eager to practice what you preach, to put your. . . uh, money where your mouth is, so to speak."

"You are joking, right?" My voice began to rise. "You aren't assuming that just because I'm here I would. . ."

"No, I'm not assuming. . . . My dear, I am a tired old man. If you're going to start spouting jut-jawed feminist rhetoric, know right now it gives me dyspepsia. I find you attractive and want to do something about it. If a girl finds it insulting that I view her in a sexual way then she can, as Pauli so eloquently puts it, stick it in her ear."

What could I do but laugh? "Look, Sam, I'm flattered that you find me attractive. However, I am not interested in doing anything about it. I am not a girl, I am a woman, and have been for many years. I may have to remain non-judgmental when a caller confesses to a delight in buggering canaries, but I don't have to be non-judgmental in my personal life, and I'm not."

Sam's moustache twitched in annoyance. "I. . . " he began.

"I have a great many judgments against being patronized," I went on, "And against even the joking implication that by acknowledging my interest in sex I, or any other woman, may be assumed to have round heels!"

"Round heels?" Sam snorted. "That expression is even older than my etchings." He turned away muttering, "Female persons! His or *her* problem! His or her *penis*, for Christ's sake!"

"He called back!" James interrupted excitedly. "The quadraplegic. That was him I was just talking to."

"What did you tell him?" I had never seen James so animated.

"I told him to call University Media Center and ask for their book and film list on sex and disability. I asked him to phone me back next week to give me some time to find out what else might be available. Are there any resources for a man like him, Sam? Do you know? I hope I didn't get his hopes up for nothing. I was just so glad to hear from him. I was sure I'd flubbed the call."

"You might want to refer him to a therapist or a sexual surrogate experienced in working with disabled men. There are several." Sam was already riffling through the referral file.

Three people from the evening shift came in together. Sam and James huddled over the file. I put on my jacket and gratefully took my leave. It had been an extremely long three hours.

3

SHAKING DOWN

Stella opened the door for me when I arrived at the Switchboard the following week. I smiled into her grave, sweet face, feeling a surge of tenderness towards her. "Hey," she greeted me. "I hear I missed James's incredible cake."

"I'm so glad you're back, Stella. How did you hear about James's cake?"

"My friend Karl worked the Thursday evening shift last week. He told me that when he got here, there was half a chocolate cake on the table, with 'V.D.' written on it in pink icing. He said he was scared to eat any—he thought that maybe the pink icing was some kind of warning. You know, like the skull and crossbones on a bottle of cleaning fluid." She burst into a peal of giggles.

I laughed with her.

"I've heard people swear that they caught V.D. from a toilet seat, or even from trying on clothes, but chocolate cake? That's new."

"Well, I got mine in the usual way," Stella said. "That's why I wasn't here last week. I had a flare-up of my vaginal herpes. I was much too uncomfortable to sit here for three hours being sex-positive over the phone."

"How are you doing now, Stella?" I swallowed and switched instinctively to my neutral phone volunteer voice. Despite my awareness of all the unpleasant diseases being contracted by all sorts of people, genital herpes carried a charge for me that a cold sore simply did not. I had heard it called the wages of sin. "Is there anything you do for the pain?" I asked her.

"I break off a piece from an aloe vera plant, and dab the sap onto the lesion," Stella answered. "It stings, but it seems to help the sore heal faster. If I feel a lesion coming on, sometimes I can keep it from breaking out by applying ice to the spot. Unfortunately, it didn't work this time."

"Stella, please. . ." Sam came out of the kitchen. "Be very careful what you tell a caller with herpes," he said seriously. "Plant juices or ice may work for you, but some guy standing around with his dick in a bucket of melting ice cubes is going to be very pissed off at the Switchboard (if he can piss anything but icicles) when his lesions don't clear up. We've got to make sure to give out only factual information here. Old wives' tales won't do."

I was pleased to notice the firm set of Stella's jaw. "I said it sometimes works for me and that's exactly what I'd tell a caller," Stella retorted. "I subscribe to the newsletter of the herpes research group and I've done some research on my own. I know there's no known cure. I've had this damn thing on and off since I was fifteen, and if someone told me that I'd get rid of it permanently by eating porcupine poop, I'd eat some. I plan to keep on telling callers what I know to be true for me, if that's all right with you"

"Okay, Stella, sorry if I sounded officious—I just worry about the Switchboard's reputation for being factual, that's all. I know that herpes can hurt like a sonofabitch. Okay? Friends?" Stella tossed her braids back over her shoulders. "Sure," she shrugged.

Sam gave her one of his ritual pats, walked back to his desk, and put his feet up. The phone rang, Sam answered it, and we were back to business as usual.

It's Hard Growing Up

Sam: Sex Information. . .

Caller: What's a boner?

S: A boner? That's what it's called when a guy's penis gets hard. Sometimes it's called an erection, a hard-on, or a stiff. Have you ever heard it called any of those things?

C: I don't think so. Does it happen to girls too?

S: Girls don't have penises. They have a clitoris—a sex organ located in about the same place as a man's penis. It's much smaller than a penis—about the size and shape of a pea—so when it gets hard, it isn't as noticeable as a hard penis.

C: How come that happens?

S: The clitoris or the penis getting hard?

C: Yeah.

S: A boy's penis gets hard when he gets sexually excited, turned-on. Sometimes just thinking about something sexy might do it. Sometimes it gets hard because something rubs against it, like his pants, or the bedsheet. Sometimes, especially with teenaged boys, it gets hard for no particular reason. Some boys get pretty embarrassed when that happens. Has it ever happened to you?

C: Kind of. It sort of gets hard when I rub it.

S: Yes, that does happen. May I ask how old you are?

C: Uh. . . I'm nineteen.

S: Really? You sound much younger to me. You know, no matter how old you are, I'll still talk with you. You don't have to be any special age to have questions about sex, or about changes in your body. I've talked to some kids as young as six.

C: I'm older than that. I'm 11. . . Is that okay?

S: It's okay with me if it's okay with you. Is there something more you want to ask?

C: My older brother says I shouldn't rub myself.

S: He says you shouldn't rub your penis?

C: My what?

S: What do you call what you have between your legs?

C: My dick.

S: Penis is another word for dick. There are lots of names for it. You said your brother told you that you shouldn't rub your dick?

C: Yeah. He says I'm too young to get a boner and I didn't know what a boner was. You say that's when my dick gets hard. Well, mine sort of does when I rub it.

S: Does it feel good to you when you do that?

C: It feels kind of funny.

S: That funny feeling is arousal, a sexual feeling. It happens to everyone—boys and girls, men and women.

C: Am I too young to do it?

S: What do you think?

C: Well, I do it.

S: There's your answer. What you do—rubbing yourself to feel good—is called masturbation, playing with yourself.

C: Umm. . . do you do it, Mister?

S: Yes I do. I've been masturbating since I was about your age. Even when I was married I did it. I still do.

C: I don't think my mom would like it if she knew I did it.

S: Has she said so?

C: No, but I just know she wouldn't.

S: A lot of grownups feel embarrassed about sexual things. They're uncomfortable talking about sex, or even certain parts of the body. Masturbation—touching yourself to feel good—is one of the things people can feel very uncomfortable talking about. It's something most people do in private and they feel private about it.

C: Is it bad, then?

S: Nothing bad will happen to a person because they masturbate. It won't make them go blind or crazy, or stop them from being a mother or a father when they grow up.

C: Do girls do it too?

S: Yes, some of them. And don't worry about doing it too much, either. Your body will tell you when to stop—you just won't feel like doing it for a while.

C: It's okay to play with yourself then?

S: That's up to you. Some people think that it's wrong or babyish or sinful, and so they feel bad about themselves after they do it. How do you feel about it?

C: I don't know.

S: Well, let me make a suggestion. There are some very good books written for people your age about teenagers and sex— about the changes your body will be going through as you grow into a man. You can get them at the public library, or in paperback at a book store. Read one, and see if that will give you a better idea of what goes on with boys and men.

C: Okay

S: Now, do you want to talk some more, or have I given you enough to think about for a while?

C: Nah, that's okay.

S: Remember, you can call us again any time with more questions. There's nothing wrong with wanting to know about your body at any age.

C: Yeah, okay. Bye.

As Sam hung up, James said pensively, "You know, Sam, I never heard that term used to mean a hard-on. Where I come from, a boner is a mistake."

"A lot of times it still is," Sam said dryly, and they both chuckled.

The next call I took seemed to prove that point.

Birth Control Is For Every Conceivable Occasion

Caller: I want to ask you a question about those baby pills.

Isadora: Baby pills. You mean like baby aspirin, the flavored kind?

C: Nah. Them pills you take if you don't want none.

I: Birth control pills. Is that what you mean?

C: I guess so. They give me them at the clinic when I had my last baby and tell me to take one every morning if I don't want no more babies for a while.

I: Yes, those are called birth control pills. How long ago did you start taking them? When was your baby born?

C: It's four months now.

I: Are you nursing the baby?

C: Nah, my momma takes care of her and my two little boys. I gotta go to school.

I: I asked because it's not good to take birth control pills if you're breastfeeding.

C: Yeah. Well. . .

I: You had a question about the pills.

C: Yeah. My older boy got into my purse. He was playin' with the dial on the dohiky those pills came in, and he mess it up. There might could be some missing.

I: Missing? Did your little boy eat some, do you think? If he did, they might make him sick. Does he seem okay to you?

C: Oh, he fine. But I think I might've forgot to take some.

I: Well. . . all right, let's see. Do you know when your last period was?

C: 'Bout two weeks ago.

I: Do you know the exact date?

C: Nah.

I: How often do you take your pills? Every day? Or do you stop taking them for a few days each month?

C: Every day.

I: Okay. With that type of birth control pill, if you miss one pill you can take two the next day. If you miss two pills, you can take two a day for the next two days. If you miss three or more it's best to stop completely, wait for your period to come, and then start all over. Since you don't know how many you missed, or *if* you missed any. . .

C: Couldna been no more than two or three.

I: Well, my suggestion would be to continue to take whatever pills are left, but to use another different kind of birth control for the rest of the month—some other way to keep yourself from getting pregnant.

C: How I do that?

I: Do you have a regular sexual partner? Husband? Boyfriend?

C: Do I have a man?

I: Do you have one main man or more than one?

C: I just seeing the baby's daddy now.

I: Could you not have sex with him for the rest of the month? Intercourse, I mean.

C: (Laughter) You gotta be kiddin'.

I: If that's not possible, would he be willing to wear a rubber?

C: No way.

I: It's only for about two weeks.

C: Uh uh.

I: There are other birth control methods. You can buy birth control foam in a drugstore, and spray it inside your vagina before you have sex. Or they have suppositories, like big pills that you put inside you each time you have intercourse.

C: I don't have no money to be messin' with junk like that.

I: Maybe the clinic that gave you the birth control pills can give you something else to use until you get your next period.

C: I called them, and they gimme a appointment in three weeks. They said to call you folks to find out what to do in the meantime.

I: Well, I don't know what else to tell you. If you did miss several pills, there's a real possibility that you could get pregnant if you have intercourse within the next couple of weeks. So here are your choices: You could ask your man not to put his dick inside you when you have sex; or you could use foam or suppositories, or your man could use a rubber. Any other birth control methods must be gotten through your clinic.

C: Shit.

I: I'm really sorry. I wish I could do more to help. Believe me, I don't like these birth control methods any more than you do. But that's all there is right now. Let me give you the number of a Planned Parenthood clinic near you? Hello?

"Damn! I shook my head and turned to Stella. "She's still in school, she's got three kids, and her little boy might be growing breasts. She laughs at the idea that her man might cooperate in the venture of not making babies for two weeks, and she's mad at me because I can't solve her problem," I fumed.

"Breeders!" James mumbled.

"What?" I asked him.

"That's what gays call straights sometimes," James explained.

"That's ridiculous," Stella piped up. "Someone has to breed if there's gonna be any gay people or any people at all! I mean, James, that's homosexist, is what it is."

My mind was still on the frustrating phone call. "I sure do wish," I sighed, "that the process were different, that there was a magic pill we would take to get pregnant and not have to think about it the rest of the time."

"I'm glad my wives didn't have access to that pill," Sam called from the bathroom. "I like to feel needed, and I like making babies."

The Merry May Fiddle, The Gay May Dance.

James: Sex Information

Caller: I've been curious about something. Can you tell me — What do gay people do?

J: You mean sexually?

C: Yeah.

J: They do everything any two people do—hug, kiss, cuddle, touch, lick, rub.

C: Yeah, but what do they usually do?

J: There is no usual. If they're both men, they can also have anal intercourse. If they're both women, they can do everything a woman and a man can do without a penis. Or if they want to, they can use an artificial penis, a dildo. But then, so could anybody else.

C: Don't gay guys always do it in the ass?

J: No. And by the way, many straight people do it that way too. Anal sex isn't just a homosexual activity. Gay men don't always have oral sex—suck cocks—either. Both men might want to have anal or oral sex or masturbate together or they might take turns. It's very individual.

C: How do they tell who does what to who? Isn't there a masculine one and a feminine one?

J: Not necessarily. How do a man and a woman decide who is going to be on top?

C: I'm always on top. The man is always on top.

J: That may be true for you, but it isn't true for every couple. The woman can be on top sometimes, or the couple can be side by side. There are lots of different positions for having sex.

C: What can two women do without a penis?

J: All the things I said. Most Lesbians are sexual with other women because they like women and women's bodies. If they wanted a penis they'd have to relate to the man it was attached to. When two women are together, they use fingers, hands, mouth, knees, anything, in the same way you might use your fingers, mouth or penis. Or they could use a dildo or a vibrator. Vibrators aren't just for Lesbians, by the way.

C: Isn't it true that Lesbians just go with women if they can't get a man?

J: Not at all. Is that why you like women?

C: Of course not. Women turn me on.

J: That's true for Lesbians, too. Many of them have been married or have had sex with men. Some Lesbians continue to have sex with men. They identify as Lesbians usually because they *prefer* women, not because they hate men or can't get one, or because they want to *be* one. By the way, all Lesbians are not masculine-looking, and all gay men are not effeminate.

C: I've never met a Lesbian or a gay man.

J: I absolutely guarantee that you have. But if they don't fit the stereotype of what you think a gay person looks like, and they don't tell you they're gay, how would you know?

C: Why would someone prefer their own sex?

J: I can't tell you that. No one knows. Some theories say people are born that way. Some say it has to do with early upbringing or life experiences. Sometimes it's a personal or political choice. In some cultures at some times it's been okay to be a homosexual. In other cultures homosexuals have been hounded and killed for their sexual orientation. All we know for sure is that there have always been homosexual people and there probably always will be, whether society approves or not.

C: What goes on in the gay districts like Castro Street?

J: Everyday living. Going to the store, walking the dog, going out to dinner or a movie or dancing. What's also going on is people connecting with other people. Exactly what goes on in any neighborhood. People are not strolling around naked or screwing on the sidewalks there.

C: What about the Gay Freedom Day Parade?

J: That's a time for gays and Lesbians and their friends to be together, demonstrate their beliefs, celebrate who they are.

Some have serious political concerns, some just want to have a good time. All the people who march on St. Patrick's Day aren't Irish. Some of the people who march in the Gay Day Parade are friends of gay people, or their children, spouses, or parents, demonstrating their support.

C: I'd hate it if a kid of mine was gay.

J: What about if he or she was a Moonie, or hard-of-hearing, or funny-looking?

C: I'd hate that too.

J: And . . . ? We all want the best possible life for those we love. Being gay or Lesbian in our society isn't easy. But if a child is other than what you would want them to be, what can you do? Love them anyway, I'd hope.

C: Yeah, I guess.

J: Have I answered your questions? Do you have something more you want to talk about?

C: Not for now. Oh yeah, what are you?

J: What am I?. . . A man.

C: Yeah, I thought so. You have a deep voice.

James hung up the phone, but he looked uncertain. I thought he'd handled a potentially hostile call very well, and I told him so.

James shook his head at me. "I feel like I copped out," he said.

"In what way?" Now I was perplexed.

"That guy asked me what I am. I said 'a man.'"

Now what? I asked myself. If 6'6", 250-pound James Hoover was about to tell me he was a woman in drag, I was going to hear it without blinking. I took a deep breath and asked cautiously, "Aren't you? A man, I mean?"

"You know what he meant as well as I do," James said, with some irritation. "When I said 'a man,' he obviously took that to mean a heterosexual man, a *normal* man in his book."

"But he was, in fact talking to a man," Sam said emphatically. "So how did you cop out? You told him the truth."

James looked intently at Sam. "Sam, I'm a gay man. Don't you think that's a relevant detail, considering the points I was making?"

I silently gave myself some credit for not having jumped to a conclusion about James's sexual orientation when he'd said that he was a nurse. I was pleased that it had never even occured to me.

"And I repeat," Sam continued, "that he was talking to a man, as stated. What you choose to reveal about your personal life to a caller is your own business."

James's lips quirked in a crooked smile. "Where I grew up you weren't considered a man until you'd wrestled a steer and slept with a woman."

"And so. . ." Sam prompted.

"Hell, I didn't sleep with anyone until I was thirty-one years old." James sidestepped. "And then it wasn't a woman," he added softly.

"How old are you now?" I asked in surprise.

"Thirty-three," James answered gravely. "I have wrestled some big ol' farm animals, but by home-town standards I. . . uh, still don't qualify."

Stella broke the uncomfortable silence which followed by twining her arms around James's bulky body and whispering, in her sexy little girl whisper, "Do you want to do something about that?"

"I was going to suggest Pauli, actually, if you're interested," Sam smiled. "Did you know that she's a sexual surrogate?"

"I didn't know that," I said to myself.

The mind boggles.

"Isadora. . . " James solemnly turned to me and I held my breath. "You neglected to mention a female lover as a birth control option to the woman with the pill problem."

"Great idea. If she calls back, I'll suggest it," I said and we all laughed in relief.

"That reminds me, James. . . ," Stella began.

"What? You forgot your birth control last night?" Sam teased.

"No." James jumped into it. "She must have forgotten it

−54−

today. Otherwise, she'd be making good her offer to make a man out of me here and now. Right, Stella?"

"No," Stella started again. "It's about Chile."

"What is?" Had I missed something in this conversation?

"James, do you have any idea whether Chile. . . likes women?" Stella finally blurted out.

"Do I have any idea? Why would I know? You think homosexuals know each other at a glance?" James teased her. "You were in the same training session—the one Chile spoke at—that I was in. You know him as well as I do. I think Chile likes *everyone*. He's one of the most loving people I've ever met."

"Sam, Isadora, do you know what his story is?" Stella would not be put off.

I shrugged. Sam shook his head. "Have you considered asking him directly?" he suggested, true to form.

"I just might," Stella mused. "Well. . . where were we? Oh, yes. James?" she smiled brightly, and repeated. "Do you want to change your luck? I'm available."

James looked distinctly uncomfortable, and for a moment remained silent. "I can't stand the suspense!" Sam roared. "Do you or do you not want to fuck?"

"Sam," I laughed, "do you extend that invitation to all the new volunteers?" Sam shot me a withering look. Oops. . .

James smiled with relief, "How about a back massage instead, Stella? Remember, I'm a very slow starter."

Stella deftly arranged James's body in the middle of the floor and started to work on his shoulders. When I left at six o'clock, I had to step over his outstreached leg on my way to the door.

4

COMING TOGETHER

The following Sunday afternoon I went by myself to a bar with live country and western music. It was not unusual for me to go out alone, but it wasn't generally my first choice. So I was relieved to see a familiar black hat bobbing high above the sea of other cowboy hats of varied hue filling the crowded Rainbow Cattle Company. James waved when he saw me and insisted, in pantomine, that I take his stool at the bar. Conversation was impossible in the hubub of electric fiddle, twanging guitars, stomping boots, and busy bottle-clanking at the bar. For almost thirty minutes we sat companionably sipping our beers and watching the action. Occasionally I caught him glancing at me, but when I looked back inquiringly, he indicated the noise level with hand to ear, and didn't attempt any conversation.

When the band took its break, James lowered himself to the now empty stool beside mine. "What a surprise to see you, Isadora. What are you doing in a gay bar?" he asked in amusement.

"Same as you. Listening to the music."

"I'm also checking out the cowboys," he admitted with a grin.

"So am I," I grinned back.

At my prompting, he told me a little about the small Wyoming cow town where he was born and raised, his lonely childhood, the aura of cowboy machismo that pervaded life there. He admitted to feeling both vengeful and vindicated watching the moustached and booted banes of his youth dancing cheek to whiskered cheek here in this big city replica of his hometown saloon. "It's just like back home," he shook his head, "and also, boy, it's not like back home! It's culture shock in spades, and it tickles me."

Our conversation stopped when the band began again. I danced a few times with men when asked, and once with a short, bosomy, blonde woman who reminded me startlingly of my mother. The main thing that felt odd was dancing with someone not quite my own height. At 5'3" that hadn't happened to me since Junior High School. The soft squoosh of breast against breast as she expertly led me in a Western Waltz brought to mind a family friend of my girlhood, a short man with a huge belly paunch. I had leaned into and on that softness as he whirled me around my first steps on the dance floor. There really wasn't that much difference. James gave me a peck on the cheek and left when I returned from the dance floor.

A private person, no doubt out of long necessity, he made no mention of our meeting when we were next at the Switchboard. But his manner towards me, towards us all, seemed a bit more relaxed. At one point, when I was absentmindedly rubbing the muscles of my neck after a long phone call, James came up behind me, and with a polite "May I?" began to knead my shoulders with one huge hand, gently lifting the hair off my neck with the other. Sam raised an eyebrow and I leaned back against James with a sigh of pleasure. I closed my eyes and ignored Sam, his moustache and his eyebrow.

I was sorry when James removed his hands to answer the phone. I had hoped that Stella would take the call.

That Hit The Spot

Caller: My lover was telling me that they've discovered some new sexually sensitive spot on women's bodies that gives them better orgasms. Do you people know anything about that?

James: Yes, sir. Are you talking about the Grafenberg spot, the G spot?

C: I suppose so. What is it?

J: It's been called the female prostate. Some researchers have identified it as an area about the size of a nickel located deep in the vaginal wall about two inches inside and toward the front of the body; sort of along the path of the urethra.

C: Okay, but what is it exactly? What does it do?

J: When that area is stimulated by hand or in certain intercourse positions it's supposed to trigger orgasms in some women, and sometimes even, so I'm told, ejaculation of a fluid.

C: Women ejaculate?

J: So they say.

C: I've never heard of such a thing.

J: There are women who report a definite spurt of liquid when they climax. Some of them thought that the orgasm caused a loss of bladder control, and that the liquid must be urine. Other women believed that the contractions of the vaginal walls during orgasm pushed out lubricating fluid. Chemical tests show that this fluid is neither lubricating secretions nor urine though it does come out of the urethra. It's more like spermless semen than anything else. But only a certain number of women say this happens to them. The research is very new. Maybe as it's popularized in the media, more women will report experiencing it.

C: But women's bodies have been women's bodies since the beginning of time. How come such an important discovery is just being investigated now?

J: Who knows? Times change. There are still books in print which say that most women have no sexual feelings whatsoever, or no desires, or no fantasies. These were popular beliefs in recent times. There have always been reports of women ejaculating or liking some special spot which wasn't the clitoris rubbed in a certain way. Now some public notice is being taken of what these people have been saying.

C: How can I find the miraculous spot?

J: Have you asked your lover? Is she a woman, by the way?

C: Yes, my lover is a woman. When female lovers were called mistresses there was no confusion, was there? She's the one who told me about the G spot, but she says she can't seem to locate hers by herself. I'm delighted to help, but I haven't the slightest idea where to look or what to look for. I could be poking around in there for days — not that she'd mind, I'm sure.

J: All right, try this. Ask her to lie face down on the bed with her legs apart and her hips slightly elevated. If she's somewhat turned on it would make things easier, but I know it's hard to be clinical and sexual simultaneously.

C: I can be one, she can be the other.

J: All right. Insert two fingers into her vagina, palm facing downward, and feel deeply a few inches inside toward the part of her body facing the bed. Stroke that whole area between the pubic bone and the cervix with a firm pressure. Have a towel handy since some women feel an urgent need to urinate when that area is massaged.

C: No problem.

J: You might want to stimulate her in other ways at the same time. Or she could do it, play with her clitoris or touch her nipples, I mean. The G spot, if she has one, should swell. . .

C: You mean some women don't have one?

J: So it seems. No one really knows how many women do. But if your partner does, it will swell as she gets more excited and that'll make it easier to feel. If you both want to have intercourse, rear entry into the vagina is a good position for stimulating the area too. Another position that some say works well is to have the woman seated on top of the man. Once you're inside she's going to have to guide you, either verbally or by body reactions. Don't be discouraged if you can't be sure you've found it the first couple of times you try. She may not recognize the feeling, but many women say that's it definitely there and worth finding, that it's worth some effort.

C: Sounds more like fun than effort to me. But let's say we find it and Nirvana at the same time. Aren't we back to that old Freudian bugaboo about clitoral vs. vaginal orgasms? Is there a difference? Is one kind "better" in some way?

J: How can I say?

C: It must be nice for jaded people, who thought they knew everything there was to know about sex, to discover that there's a new wrinkle they hadn't heard about.

J: Spot, not wrinkle.

C: Oh, right.

J: There's a sex educator on the Switchboard Training Staff named Peter Brown. He says that it's very lucky for the women of the world that he was not the discoverer of the Grafenberg spot.

C: Why is that?

J: I kinda hoped you would ask that. He says, "Who would go through all that trouble searching for something called the Brown Spot?"

C: (Laughter) Right you are. Thanks for your help, and I'm sure my lover will thank you even more.

"That was a great explanation, James," I said when he smilingly hung up the phone. "I must admit that several times since the Training I've gone exploring on my own. I've been in practically up to my elbow, but no luck. That damn thing, if it's there, is as elusive as the Fountain of Youth."

"Would you like me to help you look?" Stella offered. "I have a speculum in my bag."

"No, thank you, Stella," I blushed, and, forestalling any other forthcoming offers of assistance, I added, "and no thank you, Sam."

Sam looked offended. "I wasn't about to offer. You had your chance."

James smoothed over the awkward moment by chuckling

to himself. "The Brown Spot. I forgot about that until I took this call. I liked that guy who called. He sounded so intelligent and cheerful about sex. That was a really nice change."

"If he calls back ever, see if you can interest him in becoming a volunteer," Stella brightened. "We can always use more cheerful intelligence around here." She glanced mischievously at Sam, who ignored her. She winked at me and answered the next phone that rang.

It's All In The Head

Stella: Sex Information.

Caller: What's it like having a penis in your mouth?

S: What is it like?

C: Have you ever done that?

S: Many times, but what it's like for me wouldn't be the same for someone else. Are you asking about your penis or your mouth or both?

C: I. . . geez, it's hard to say this.

S: Are you asking what it might be like for you to suck a cock?

C: Damn, that's really laying it out there!

S: Have you ever had your own cock sucked?

C: Yes.

S: How did you feel about the person who did it to you? Was it a man or a woman, by the way?

C: A woman. I only have sex with women.

S: Well, how did you feel about what she did?

C: I was surprised. . .grateful, I guess. Here was this woman willing to. . .I mean, I didn't even ask her to. See, this woman seemed to want. . .she seemed to be enjoying it as much as I was. She even said afterward, "I love to suck cock," like I might say I love to go rollerskating! I never thought that. . .I don't know how to put it.

S: It sounds to me like you've always thought of it as an unexpected favor someone might do for you rather than something that feels good to the person who's doing it, too. Is that right?

C: Yes. There is something. . . well, very personal about putting your mouth where someone else pisses. Like who would *want* to do that?

S: Have you ever gone down on a woman?

C: No. I've never wanted to, and fortunately, no one's ever asked me to.

S: And so you thought no one would want to do it to you, right?

C: Yes. But this woman did, on her own. She *liked* it.

S: I like it too. Many people do. I also like going down on women.

C: Are you a lez', or what?

S: I'm a "what", I guess. I consider myself heterosexual, and I sometimes have sex with women. I guess most people would label me bisexual.

C: I thought a person had to be one or the other.

S: Nope. Anyway I'm not one or the other and there are lots of others like me out there.

C: Yeah, way out there.

S: Back to you, though. What was the question you asked me originally?—How does it feel to suck a cock? I can't really answer that except to say some people like it, some people hate it. . . For many it depends on whose cock it is, and how they feel about that person. You said you weren't interested in going down on a woman. Do you want to talk about going down on a man?

C: Whew. I don't know.

S: It bothers you to talk about it, or to think about doing it?

C: Well. . . to even talk about thinking about it is. . . queer.

S: You mean queer like gay, or queer like who would ever want to put his mouth where someone else pees from?

C: Both, I guess.

S: It seems that oral sex in general is an unpleasant idea for you but that oral sex with a man is somehow worse.

C: For me it would be much worse.

S: Because cocks are worse than pussies?

C: Because. . . the only people who suck cock are either women or fags.

S: And neither a woman nor a fag is as good a thing to be as a straight man, is that what you're saying?

C: I don't think I mean that. . . exactly.

S: It sounds to me like you're saying that to suck a cock would make you less of a man, that it's degrading to anyone, but especially to a *man*.

C: I'd be a cocksucker!

S: Yeah, I guess you would. That sure is a heavily loaded word. There's a joke I heard once: A cranky old man is talking about his life to another old man and he says, "You know, I had four children. No one ever called me Jack, the father. I was in business for 50 years. No one ever called me Jack, the businessman. But just suck one cock. . . "

C: I don't get it.

S: Never mind. Maybe I didn't tell it right. Let's get back to that loaded word, cocksucker, and talk about your feelings about the queer people who do it.

C: Are you making fun of me?

S: Nope. Does it sound that way to you?

C: I don't know what I'd be if. . .

S: What would you be if you went down on a woman?

C: A better lover?

S: (laughing) For sure, in my book. What are your feelings about oral sex in general? It's unclean, queer, what else?

C: I know it feels good to get it. . .

S: Okay. For many people that's true. But for some people receiving it doesn't feel good either. Either because the one who is doing it is rough or awkward, or because the whole idea is so embarrassing and uncomfortable there is just no way they can relax and enjoy the good feelings.

C: How do you, how does anyone, do it well?

S: I'm going to start at the beginning. For many people—men and women and any combination of them—it's a regular part of their sexual expression. So it's not odd for a great number of people; it's normal for them. Cleanliness *is* a real consideration for many folks. But mouths are actually the most bacteria-filled orifices of the human body. People don't seem to be bothered by that when they kiss. You could shower or bathe with a person before having sex, or wipe around the genitals with a warm wash cloth as part of sex play. If you have a lot of your own saliva in your mouth before you touch it to another person's genitals, their taste and smell will seem more familiar to you.

C: But what exactly do I do?

S: Whatever feels good. There is no one right way to give head—to a man or to a woman. You might lick, suck, kiss, nibble gently on cunt or cock, clitoris or balls. See what you like, see what your partner responds to. When they're close to orgasm, most women and men like regular and rhythmic stimulation until they come.

C: I'm afraid I might gag.

S: Then stop. If you're going down on a woman and you need to stop, use your fingers in the same way you were using your tongue. Women in general do not like as firm a pressure on their clitorises as men do on their penises, but that's general rather than specific.

C: Okay.

S: A person of either sex might enjoy a finger or two inside at the same time, in the vagina or in the anus. When giving head to a man, you can hold the base of his cock with your hand to control just how much can go into your mouth. If you raise and lower your head to him, rather than his thrusting into your mouth, that also gives you more insurance against gagging.

C: But . . .

S: If you don't want to swallow his cum, have a tissue or towel handy to spit into. If you don't want him to come in your mouth, ask him to let you know when he's close, or watch for the signs.

C: Geez . . .

S: If you'd like to see how people do it, you might go to a porno film. Almost all of them have scenes of oral sex on both sexes.

C: I've never seen a pornographic movie.

S: Well, I'm not really recommending them. Most of them are sexist, silly, and not very realistic. Porn actors are into high drama, but you might learn some technical how-tos from them.

C: Yeah, I guess.

S: Do you want to talk about where you might find the opportunity to suck a cock?

C: Boy, woman, you sure are pushy. I'm not ready for that!

S: Okay, okay, anything else you want to ask about? Nothing?. . . Hello?

Stella turned to Sam, seated behind her at the next desk. "Do you think I'm pushy?" she demanded indignantly.

"You?" Sam smiled. "Hardly."

"The guy I was talking to just called me pushy and hung up on me. I was going to tell him about glory holes at the bars and baths, but I guess I came on too strong."

"Not everybody is as liberated as you, my dear," Sam said

with that amused paternalism which irritated me mightily, but which Stella seemed able to ignore. "You might have been a bit gentler with his sensibilities. What do you know about glory holes anyway?"

"Probably as much as you do, Sam, unless you have some secret predilections," Stella sassed him. "Now that I think of it, it's impossible to keep any personal secrets around here, isn't it? You all know that I have herpes, James was a virgin cowboy past the age of thirty, Sam has had three wives and likes busty women. Isadora . . ."

Mercifully, the phone rang and I lunged for it. If ever there was a case of "saved by the bell" . . .

On Being A Man

Caller: I'm seventeen years old and I want to know how to fuck a girl?

Isadora: Do you want to know how to persuade a girl to have sex with you, or are you asking what to do once she has agreed?

C: How do you fuck her?

I: Fucking is something you do *with* someone, not *to* her. It's not like batting a baseball. A person has to agree to have sex with you and then the two of you get together and cooperate in the activity. Do you understand what I'm saying?

C: How do you get a girl to cooperate with you?

I: For one, you might try asking her.

C: Just go up to some chick and ask her, "Do you wanna fuck?"

I: Well, that's one way. But I'm fairly sure she'd say no. Sex is one of the things two people may want to share, like their time, or their ideas, or feelings. Girls are people. This may come as a shock, but girls want the same things boys want—to be liked, accepted and approved of, to feel good about themselves.

C: How about fucking. Do they want to fuck too?

I: Sure. Many of them want that too. But many young women feel other things should come first, or are more important. Another thing is that girls are the ones who get pregnant, so they'll probably be more cautious about having all the sex they might want. Both boys and girls usually want to start having sex long before they're ready to start having babies.

C: Can't they take the pill?

I: Yes. And you can use a condom. Or you both can decide together on some other birth control method. But that doesn't change the fact that she's the one who might get pregnant, not you.

C: Well, what does a guy do if he wants to get laid?

I: There are several possibilities. One, you can pay for sex. It's against the law so it's risky, but there are people who sell sexual services.

C: You mean prostitutes? Nah, I don't wanna mess with them.

I: Then, the other choice is to find a girl who is willing to have sex with you. But you must be willing to take part of the responsibility to keep her from getting pregnant. Of course, she won't get pregnant if you are sexual with her without having intercourse. There might be more young women who would be willing to do that with you. Or you might be sexual with yourself.

C: I already jerk off, but that's really nowhere. And feeling a girl up isn't *real* sex.

I: You feel it isn't real if you don't have intercourse. It doesn't count?

C: Right. It might feel good. But it wouldn't be getting laid. Real men fuck girls.

I: Is that what your friends say?

C: Yeah.

I: Well, I know that's what some guys tell each other, but it just isn't true. Being a man means taking responsibility for what you do, being aware of other people's feelings and being honest with yourself and other people.

C: I'm being honest. I really want to get laid!

I: I believe you. Sorry if I sounded preachy. But the best way to find a sexual partner is to set up some honest communication.

C: Yeah, right, okay. Then what do I do?

I: Whatever feels good to you both. I'm not being flip. There is no one right way to fuck. Two people usually do some hugging, touching, kissing, exploring each other's bodies in ways that feel nice to each of them. What sex is about is pleasure — giving it and getting it.

C: What about blowing in a girl's ear? My friend says that always gets them hot.

I: Is that what he says? I personally hate to have anyone blow in my ear.

C: Did it get you hot when you were a teenager?

I: No. I always found it annoying.

C: Well. . . so. . . how do I know what to do then?

I: You might try asking "Does that feel good? Do you like it when I do this?" But you must know that many people, boys and girls, are often shy about saying what does feel best to them. Or they might not know, since it's so new. Or, what feels good at first might be irritating after a few minutes. A good lover learns to pay attention to body language, to happy sighs and sounds, to whether your partner is moving closer to or away from your touch, to her breathing rate. Lots of things besides words can tell you what's going on.

C: Let's get to the real part. How do I fuck?

I: I want to tell you something very important. For many girls and women the touching, holding, kissing *is* the real part. Intercourse might feel good, but they *prefer* all the other things that go with it. For them the other stuff's the best part of sex.

C: Yeah, okay, but then what?

I: When your partner is ready, she might push her pelvis against yours. She might open her legs and guide your penis into her vagina, or help you do that. Or she might show her willingness by just not doing anything to keep you from doing it yourself. She might be wet inside and around her vagina, or she might need some additional lubrication. For that, saliva will do just fine. If your penis is hard, and she's let you know that she's willing, *and* you've done something about birth control, you guide your penis into her vagina and move together and apart.

C: Are we lying down?

I: It can be done lying down, sitting up, in lots of different positions. Once you're connected remember—it's not a race to the finish. You can speed up, slow down, stop, change positions. The connection itself feels good. And once you've come, that doesn't have to mean the end of being sexual. Be sure to caress, cuddle and kiss her; be sure she's finished too. Women, girls, often don't come as quickly as boys. And often not at all during intercourse, especially if it's her first time.

C: But my cock won't be hard any more, so what do I do?

I: Whatever you did to get turned on in the first place. The touching and fondling is sometimes called foreplay, but it's just sex play. It can be and often is done during and after as well. If you think that getting laid will make you feel manly, wait and see how manly you can feel when you have a satisfied partner. . . and that can happen without fucking.

C: I have some more questions.

I: Like what?

C: I don't know.

I: I couldn't possibly answer all the questions you have now, or the ones you have even after you've had years of sexual experience. There are lots of books and magazines you can read; educational ones, not pornography. I would recommend listening to what a girl you would like to have sex with has to say about what she might enjoy. Try talking to some of your friends honestly, perhaps on a one-to-one basis. The blow-in-her-ear-and-she'll-do-anything or you're-not-a-man-until-you've-wet-your-dick nonsense is just garbage. It's wrong information.

C: Can I call you back with some more questions?

I: Absolutely. I hope you will. Give some thought to what we've talked about, okay?

C: I will. Thanks. Hey, wish me luck.

"Well, now we know an intimate secret about you too, Isadora," James nodded knowingly. I silently reviewed the conversation. Hmmm?

"You're probably what the guys call a 'hard come,'" Stella taunted.

Obviously, they'd all been listening. Something good must be on TV this afternoon for the phones to be this quiet. What had I revealed? I fervently hoped we were finished with my G spot. Was Stella going to make another offer of her handy speculum? Sam approached me with mock gravity. While I faced him in puzzled apprehension, he deftly removed my right earring. He stabbed a piece of paper on which he had scribbled something with the wire loop, and affixed the ring back in place in my ear. Stella held up a pocket mirror, but I couldn't read Sam's scrawl backwards. I removed the earring myself and read the message there: "Don't blow on me." A little snake, remarkably phallic-looking, reared its oval head.

We were all still laughing in a positive orgy of good fellowship when the first of the evening shift arrived.

5

CONNECTIONS

The following Thursday was July 4th, and the Switch-board was closed. The week after that my daughter left for summer camp, and the flurry of last minute purchases, pack-ing and goodbyes kept me too busy to come in. So three weeks had passed before I next walked up the stairs of the fad-ed blue building and into an overwhelming bear hug from James. Pauli gave me a "Ta da" fanfare, from Stella a quick squeeze, and Sam ruffled my hair—a gesture I normally hate but accepted from him then as an affectionate welcome. I missed my daughter, my best friend was out of town on vaca-tion, and my honey had just gone off in search of a grand adventure. How nice to be so warmly and affectionately welcome somewhere!

"What's new on the sexual frontier? What have I missed?" I asked in greeting.

"Kiddo, there is nothing new in sex," Pauli drawled. "Folks have been doing all of it and regretting some of it since Adam and Eve."

"And Cain and Abel!" James added.

"There's always new terminology at least," Sam said. "I bet you don't know about 'boo foo.'"

"Oh, yes I do," I said triumphantly. "It's a term for anal sex. It stands for butt fuck, to B.F., to boo foo."

"Been researching, have you?" Sam stroked his moustache.

"My teenage daughter is a great source of information." I smiled.

"Modern times!" James shook his head. "Isn't it supposed to be the other way around?"

"Actually, we trade facts and fancies. I do know some things she doesn't."

"So you say," said Sam. "I've had teenage daughters. By the way, Isadora, you missed the question of the year. I know it's only July, but I'm sure it won't be topped. Some nervous young man called in to ask if there was a cure for *impudence!*"

"That's wonderful. I can't think of anyone better able to give him a cure, Teacherman." I laughed, pleased that there seemed to be no strain between us at the moment.

"My favorite was when this woman wanted to know if condominiums are safe," Pauli cackled.

"What about the kid, the one who must have been a math major, who was worried about the amount of his 'cubic' hair?" Stella joined in.

Oh, it did feel good to be back. Not even the first call of the afternoon, which Stella took, dampened our good spirits.

You Can Please Some Of The People Some Of The Time

Stella: Sex Information. May I help you?

Caller: Who is this?

S: This is the Sex Information Switchboard. My name is Star. Can I help you?

C: Star? What kind of name is that? What kind of phone number is this? A what Switchboard?

S: We are a telephone information service. We answer questions and make referrals on matters of human sexuality.

C: Sex? My kid has been calling and talking to you people about sex? Wait until I get my hands on him.

S: I . . .

C: This phone number showed up on my telephone bill eleven times last month. Eleven! I counted them.

S: Your boy must need some information he's not getting elsewhere. We really are a good source.

C: If he needs to know something he can ask me or his father. He doesn't have to go to strangers.

S: Maybe he feels more comfortable because we *are* strangers. Being anonymous often makes it easier to talk, especially for a young person.

C: What did you tell him?

S: That depends on what he asked. We usually tell people whatever they want to know.

C: But he's only thirteen.

S: We believe if someone's old enough to ask, he's old enough to get an honest answer.

C: I don't think that's right. He's got time later to think about that kind of thing. Nobody told me anything until I was married. My husband taught me what I needed to know.

S: Is that the way you want it for your son?

C: Well, his father can tell him when the time comes. I don't like the idea of his talking to strangers about personal things. We're his parents, and it's up to us to tell him what we think is right.

S: Now that you know he's asking questions, maybe this is the time for you or your husband to have some discussions with him.

C: Do you people actually get paid to sit around and talk dirty to just anyone?

S: We don't talk dirty, we give information. And we don't get paid. This is an all-volunteer organization.

C: That's even worse! If my son calls you again, I don't want you to tell him anything, is that clear?

Stella hung up the phone and sighed. "Why does she

think it's worse to give sex information for free than to get paid?"

"One of life's little mysteries," Sam answered.

"If it were some sort of sex for pay then she would've known what to call you," I suggested.

"I think you handled her very well, Stella," James smiled.

"Boo foo?" Pauli said into the phone, tugging on my skirt and winking at me as she spoke. Apparently this was the "in" term for the month. Ah well, when I was thirteen "eat me" was considered the definitive insult, not a gracious invitation. I sat down beside Pauli and prepared to listen and learn. If anybody could make me laugh about peoples' sexual tragedies, it was Pauli.

Communication And Lubrication

. . .

Pauli: It's a slang term for anal sex, butt fucking.

Caller: I thought so. Who does that?

P: Anyone who owns an asshole can do it.

C: I've never done it.

P: Uh huh.

C: Does it really feel good?

P: Some people find it very pleasurable. All of us have a great number of sensitive nerve endings around the anus. The anus contracts during orgasm too, you know. It pulsates along with whatever else is pulsating.

C: I never noticed.

P: Have you noticed that it can feel really good to take a shit?

C: But that's having something coming out. Having something going in seems like. . . er, heading the wrong way up a one way street.

P: Great turn of phrase, but it doesn't have to be. A sphincter muscle can relax for things coming in as well as going out. May I ask about your sexual preference?

C: I'm married.

P: Yes?

C: That's not a self-explanatory statement any more, is it? Straight, 24 years old, I'm a driving instructor.

P: A driving instructor and no experience with assholes?

C: (Laughter) Not the anatomical kind, plenty of the other.

P: Have I answered your questions? Is there anything else?

C: Yes, if you don't mind taking a bit more time. I'd like to know more about. . . how to go about it, now that I have you on the phone.

P: The key to the whole process is communication and lubrication. Lots of both.

C: Huh?

P: When you have vaginal intercourse, the vagina provides its own lubrication, if all goes well. You might want to use additional jelly or cream, but nature provides at least a start in most sexually aroused women. There isn't lubrication from the anus, so it, and whatever is going into it, should be well greased.

C: Something like Vaseline?

P: A petroleum-based product isn't really a good idea, nor is anything with perfume in it. A good general rule is that anything you can put in your mouth you can put in your ass, a vegetable oil, Crisco, butter. There are several commercial lubricating preparations too—KY Jelly, Performance, Probe.

C: And the communication part?

P: First of all, consent. This is not something you'd spring on an unprepared partner. How do you and your wife feel about it? Interested? Nervous? Repelled?

C: We've never discussed it.

P: Both of you may need mental and physical preparation. After all, you may be dealing with a virgin orifice. Sphincter muscles need to be relaxed to accommodate something going in or out. If they're not, it's like trying to swallow food when you're choked up with emotion. You can massage around the anus with the head of your penis, fingers or lips and tongue. It will help if she is turned on sexually, highly aroused, like just before or just after orgasm.

C: Uh, what about. . . germs.

P: Not only germs, but odors, and shit too, so let's talk about them. Some people find body odors, particularly of those they love, very arousing. Other people must have everything squeaky clean. You know yourself and how it is with your wife.

C: We like it squeaky clean.

P: Okay, then she can douche with warm water, take an enema, and/or make sure you don't start any anal play when her bowels are full. The germs around her anus are no more treacherous than those in her mouth, if she's perfectly healthy. Still, it's best to wash whatever goes into the anus before it goes into other places. Bacteria that are normal and healthy in the digestive tract, if transferred to a vagina by your hand or cock, can cause an infection.

C: Don't worry, I'll be careful. How about positions?

P: The lucky owner of the anus being pleasured, your wife in this case, can back into or lower herself onto your penis. Having this control can help eliminate the fear of having something rammed up the ass. The mere thought of that could sure close up the old sphincters.

C: I'm not saying that I'm King Kong, but can an anus really accommodate a whole penis without pain?

P: Depends on whose anus. Relaxation is an important factor. Go slowly. Use one finger first maybe, then maybe two. Stimulate other parts at the same time. Use reassuring words if that works. Communication again. Keep checking if you're not sure: "How's that? More? Stop for a moment?" A few people can and do accommodate something as large as a fist.

C: A fist?

-76-

P: There are people into anal fist fucking. Again, that's not someone ramming a clenched fist up someone's ass. It's a slow, intimate process requiring a tremendous amount of trust. Lots of communication, lots of lubrication.

C: That's amazing.

P: Ain't Nature grand? Hey, pardon my getting personal, but you have an asshole too. This can all work for you with the added bonus that contact with the prostate gland in a male can trigger orgasms. Do you know where your prostate is?

C: I'm not sure.

P: You might try exploring on your own, about three inches or so inside your anus and towards the front. It feels firm, about the size of a walnut, and gets harder and larger before orgasm. If your wife uses her fingers, be sure she files her nails; so there're no rough edges to scratch the sensitive inner tissues. If she uses anything else, like a dildo for instance, be sure it's nonbreakable and has something graspable on the nonbusiness end. Anal sphincters are powerful, and you don't want something like a greased cucumber disappearing up your or her ass.

C: Uh, no.

P: Has all this information put you into Overwhelm?

C: I guess it has. I don't know how I feel about it.

P: Hey, I'm not advocating ass fucking. It's just one of the many sexual activities available. This anal play stuff doesn't have to be done all at one time, or at all. You might like it, might not. If you get stuck. . . figuratively, of course, call me again. My name is Pauli. Your wife might want to talk to us also if you two decide to experiment.

C: Good idea, thanks.

P: Hey, happy boo foo.

C: Happy what? Oh, yeah. Er,. . . same to you.

"That reminds me of another of my all-time favorite calls," Sam said when Pauli got off the phone. "I answered the call and the woman began the conversation by announcing, 'My husband is interested in having *annual* sex.' "

I couldn't resist, "Did you say Happy Anniversary?"

"That's exactly what I wanted to say," Sam chuckled.

"The call might have been from Mrs. Santa Claus," Stella chimed in. "Santa comes only once a year."

Pauli waved her arms in the air to get our attention, and between laughter gasped out,". . . And then it's down the chimney!"

"Welcome to the Thursday afternoon comedy hour, folks," James said in an announcer's resonating tones.

"I keep telling folks that sex can be fun." Chile's wide grin appeared in the doorway. "Hey, Stella, someone's been thinkin' on you."

"Thinking on me?"

Chile handed her a hairclip made of iridescent blue-green feathers. Stella flushed with pleasure.

"How come?" she stammered in her confusion.

"Just for so. Or because it's a nice day. I'll hang around and take you guys out for a drink after the shift, okay?" To eliminate any doubt that "you guys" meant more than Stella, Chile affectionately squeezed James's shoulder with one hand, poked Pauli's arm, smiled at me, and gave a nod to Sam, who was taking a call.

Was It Good For You Too?

Sam: Sex Information.

Caller: Is there any way to tell for sure if a woman has had an orgasm?

S: You might try asking.

C: I always do. She says these vague things like, 'I enjoyed it," or, "That was very nice."

S: Isn't that an answer?

C: But I still don't know if she came.

S: Is that important to you?

C: Sure. I want to know if I've pleased a woman, that she's satisfied. I want to be a good lover.

S: Is this woman you're speaking of your regular partner?

C: Right now she is. The last woman friend I had was a screamer. She would gasp and moan and holler.

S: And that's proof that she was having an orgasm?

C: Isn't it?

S: Not necessarily. I don't want to confuse you, but as you know, different women react differently when they're very aroused or having an orgasm. Some women react differently from one time to the next. Some women are not sure themselves whether they've come or not. Some women feel satisfied even if they don't come at all. And some women may come several times and not be satisfied.

C: Oh boy. I thought I was going to get a straightforward answer.

S: I wish I had one. Human sexual response is different every time. Even with men it's not always the same. An ejaculation is almost always preceded or followed by an orgasm, or even simultaneously accompanied by one. . . but not always. There are such things as retrograde ejaculations; that is, no fluid comes out of the end of the penis. It backs up into the bladder. So there's an orgasm, but no visible ejaculate. You can ejaculate due to manipulation of the prostate, by a doctor, for example, and not have it be accompanied by an orgasm. Some men report multiple orgasm, but only ejaculate with the first or last one.

C: But about women. . . are there some usual signs? Anything?

S: Yes, a release of tension. That's what an orgasm is. When any person is highly aroused there is an increase in heart and breathing rate. The skin may feel hot to the touch. There may be a sexual flush like a rash on certain parts of the body. There is the same "gathering" sensation in the genitals, a focusing of energy, so to speak. In men, that is usually accompanied by the hardening and enlarging of the penis to its maximum capacity. In women, it's at that point of highest excitement that the organ corresponding to the penis, the clitoris, actually seems to hide. Instead of poking out even further from under the clitoral hood, right before orgasm it withdraws. Sometimes a women's lover thinks he's doing something wrong since her "erection" seems to have disappeared, and he stops just when she most wants him to continue.

C: Damn!

S: There's another major difference between men and women. If a man gets to a certain point of arousal, he's going to come, come hell or high water. Most women need continual stimulation, right up and through orgasm. If the stimulation is altered or stopped, the orgasm is altered or stops. When they experience that gathering feeling that precedes orgasm, many women like to stop moving around and concentrate. So that someone who has been moaning and clutching you may suddenly go limp or rigid or hold her breath and stop all that activity. Again, you might conclude that she's lost interest and stop, just when her need is for you to go on.

C: I didn't know that. Now I'm beginning to wonder if any of the women I've been with have had orgasms. For Crissakes, why don't they tell a guy these things?

S: They? You mean women in general? Shyness, misinformation, eagerness to please, lots of reasons. A book called *The Hite Report,* for instance, can tell you more than you want to know about how women experience orgasm and what they want to get them there. However, if there's one woman in your bed she's the one whose orgasm is of most concern to you, no?

C: But what do I do if I keep getting these vague answers like "It was fine"? I'm not a mind reader, and I guess I'm not even a good body reader. Why won't a woman say what she wants?

S: I agree that it's frustrating. You might try asking specific questions at a time when you're both relaxed and feeling close, maybe over dinner. Be really specific, like "When you're close to coming could you grasp my arm in a certain way so I know to keep doing what I'm doing" or "What's happening with you when you suddenly arch your back? Are you coming or just changing position?"

C: That would certainly spice up the meal!

S: If she finds these questions embarrassing or difficult to answer, you might try telling her what's going on with you. Tell her how you are feeling or what turns you on.

C: You want to join us for dinner and help me out?

S: I'm sure you'll do just fine without me. You might ask her to describe her sensations during arousal and orgasm and try to interpret the body language which expresses those feelings. You could also ask her to bring herself to orgasm and watch how and what she does.

C: I could ask . . .

S: You don't sound very optimistic. It's true that this kind of discussion is extremely difficult for some people—did you say this is a new relationship?

C: Sort of.

S: Then it may take time for your partner to trust you, to trust herself with you. Some men seem to insist on their partner's orgasms as a sort of trophy. A woman may resent this conquering attitude—"I won, I made you come"—so much that she can't or won't relax enough to have an orgasm. That kind of subliminal battle is a no-win situation for both people, but it's rarely a conscious choice—"I'm not going to give him the victory of my orgasm; that will show him who's boss."

C: I don't power-trip her.

S: Okay, if you assure her of her desirability, of your eagerness to share pleasure with her, then you might find her more forthcoming. . . no pun intended. If she still says everything is fine, believe her. Relax and enjoy yourself. Maybe she is enjoying sex with you—orgasm or no.

C: I guess that's all I can do. Thanks for your suggestions.

"Damn, Sam, that was really good." I was impressed. "Thank you, Madam."

"Really, Sam," I didn't want to drop it, "you put that very well, very clearly and directly. I never knew how women's body language came across until I saw some of the films in Training. Other than porn films where women always seem to be grinning and licking their lips, how could I know what other women did in bed except through men's reports?"

"You might sleep with a few yourself," Stella said.

I blushed at the obvious. I hadn't realized how strong a heterosexual worldview I still held.

"There are always mirrors," Pauli suggested mildly.

Later in a nearby cafe over a pizza and several carafes of wine, the six of us kicked around men/women stuff until almost 9:30. Pauli and I caught each other's eye and smiled when Stella, with childlike directness, put her hand in Chile's and leaned her head against his shoulder. We could intellectually discuss every little pre-orgasmic tingle, but the miracle of a blossoming attraction between two people was always that—a miracle. Chemistry triumphant over physics.

James walked Pauli and me to our cars. The last thing I heard was Sam's voice calling out in the darkness, "Pauli, did I tell you the difference between a rooster and a prostitute? The rooster clucks defiance . . ."

6

RELATIONSHIPS

Pauli met me outside the building the following week, puffing up the hill and waving some keys in the air. "Sam called me to say he won't be in today," she gasped. "He's doing personal research."

"For a paper? Does he write?"

Pauli shrugged. "He probably means he's off fucking all afternoon, actually."

"Now that's real dedication to the field of sexology," I laughed, relieved to know that Sam was getting laid somewhere. . . else.

"Yeah, such altruism. I get out of bed to come here to answer the phones so Sam can get off the phones to go somewhere to get into bed. As the world turns. Anyone else here?"

"Pauli, I'm standing here because no one answered the buzzer when I rang. If either James or Stella is here they're not letting on, or in."

"Maybe they're doing some personal research," Pauli waggled her eyebrows and unlocked the front door. "And if they are, I'd sure like to watch. Wouldn't you?"

I was mentally trying to think of some positions which would accommodate the vast difference in their respective sizes and body masses when James arrived. Moments later,

Stella puffed up the hill carrying a large bakery box under her arm. We all trooped up the stairs together.

"Chile sent these," Stella said, opening the box and putting a dozen doughnuts on a plate from the kitchen. I smiled to myself. Good, they were seeing each other.

"He probably thinks you need some additional cushioning, Stella," James said. When Stella's eyes widened in dismay he amended, "I mean, the chairs here are not well padded."

"And the rest of us are, you mean?" Pauli growled.

"I think I'll escape to the phones, if you. . . ladies will excuse me. I'll get into less trouble speaking with a run-of-the-mill hostile caller."

Who's In Charge Around Here?

James: Sex Information.

Caller: What do the S and M stand for in S & M?

J: S & M? It usually means sadism and masochism. It could sometimes mean slave and master as well. Is there something particular you want to know about it?

C: I'm. . . not sure. Do I have to have a specific question? I'd like you to. . . just tell me about it. Can you do that?

J: I'm willing to talk about it with you. What I don't want is to give a lecture. I'm not very good at that. Please interrupt me with any questions as they occur to you, okay?

C: Yes, thanks. I'm not. . . I mean I'm not asking you to entertain me, you know? It's. . . I. . . well, I just want to hear about it, but I don't know what I want to know, if you know what I mean.

J: Okay, look. I'll talk about S & M in a consenting and sexual setting. "Sadism" and "masochism" are used nonsexually as well, like "sadistic" drowning of kittens. When a woman becomes pregnant with her third unwanted child by a man who abuses her, I'd call that masochism. . . but she might call it God's will, or true love. S & M activity is usually. . . uh, well, a fantasy play between consenting adult sexual partners, sort of a negotiated drama of power dynamics and sexual surrender.

C: Wait a minute—That's a mouthful! What are you talking about?

J: Look, your boss says "Do this or you'll lose your job" that's an exercise of power which your boss might enjoy, but you don't, right? You can do whatever it is, resentfully, or you can quit and be without a job.

C: Okay.

J: In a different setting, your lover might say, "I'll only have sex with you in the missionary position every third Thursday from six until seven." If you want to continue to see that person and they refuse to negotiate, you are in the same powerless position; like it, lump it, or leave. These power struggles go on all the time between people. In S & M they are just brought out in the open and made into a little drama like a stage play. One person is saying, "Make me do what I want to do anyway," or "Do with me what you will; I am in your power,". . . within certain limits. You would only want to play such games with someone who can be trusted to observe your limits.

C: I think I see what you mean.

J: If you allow your sexual partner to tie you up, for example, a little human macrame, you might expect to have things done to your body that will please you sexually. If a burglar entered your home and tied you up, your expectations would be different, right? Both situations may involve rope and the element of fear, but only one is sexual *and* consenting.

C: Is that what people doing S & M stuff do—tie each other up?

J: That's one popular form. It's called bondage. There could be many other activities involved: verbal abuse, spanking, humiliation, pissing, tatooing, body piercing, wearing costumes—special underwear, rubber, or leather—whipping, pinching, to name a few.

C: Some of those things sound terribly painful.

J: Well, S & M has to do with pleasure and pain as well as power. Realize that when a person is sexually aroused, some things which usually hurt, don't. You may have noticed bite marks or scratches on your body the morning after having passionate sex, with no idea when they happened.

C: Yeah.

J: If someone standing next to you in an elevator bit your neck, you'd probably yell in anger and pain. It's not sexy in that situation. But it could be very sexy in another.

C: I guess so.

J: There is that fine line for people who play S & M games. Just exactly when certain behavior is arousing, with whom, under just what conditions, varies. You have to trust your partner if you're going to play games you feel are dangerous (physically or psychologically) and yet that element of danger, of testing limits, is also a necessary part of the fantasy. That's it, I guess, a balance between danger and responsible behavior. I never put it that way before, but it sounds right to me.

C: How could a person make this all happen?

J: Are you asking me how you could make it happen for you?

C: Yeah, I guess I am.

J: Tell me something about yourself. I'm sure we'll come up with some ideas.

C: I'm a guy, I guess you got that. I'm twenty, a student at State. I go out with girls.

J: What do you want to happen when you go out with a girl, as opposed to what does happen?

C: I'm not sure. The girls I date I mostly meet at school. Some are nice. Some are sexier than others. I don't have a lot of experience, but I'm not a virgin.

J: Uh huh.

C: Well, like. . . there's this older woman in my Lit class. She's probably around thirty. She asked me to have coffee with her after class Tuesday and I was really surprised. I never even noticed her before. Over coffee she was. . . well, coming on to me, and finally she asked me if I wanted to come home with her. I didn't know what to say. I guess she got insulted that I didn't say yes right off. She got up and said, "If you don't want to, then you don't. I'm not into S & M and I'm not going to force you," and she walked out.

J: And that got you to thinking . . .

C: I just sat there; then I realized I had a hard-on. I mean, she's already gone but now I'm turned on to her. And what did it was her saying, "I'm not going to force you." I realized that was just what I wanted her to do, just say "You look good to me. I'm taking you home with me right now and we're going to have hot sex the way I like it, whether you want to or not."

J: You wanted her to take charge.

C: Yes, exactly. Is that S & M? I mean, I wasn't thinking of whips or chains or anything that kinky.

J: You just wanted the woman to take over and run things.

C: Yes. Is that S & M?

J: Is it to you?

C: Well, you were talking about power. I realize that with the women I usually go out with it's up to me, all of it, always. I ask for the date, I make the moves. All they have to do is say yes or no. I was so blown away by having a woman come on to *me* that I didn't figure out until it was too late that I really liked that. It turned me on. I guess I don't always want to be in charge just because I'm a male.

J: I can really relate to that. I'm a very big man, and people seem to assume that I'll be the one to take charge—a big, capable authority figure in control of everything. But there are times I want to be gentled, coaxed, given directions. "Hey, I'm off duty as a caretaker. You take care of me for a change." I look like a top, I generally am a top. . . and occasionally I want to be topped for a change of pace.

C: What's that?

J: A top? Sorry. That's an S & M word too—top and bottom, dominant and submissive.

C: That's it! I want to be with a dominant woman. A socially assertive one at least. I'm not sure about the sex part.

J: Okay, now what are you going to do about that?

C: I guess I could wait and see if this woman asks me again, but I doubt she will.

J: That's being *too* passive. What else could you do?

C: I could go to places where there are agressive women, like professional organizations or women's hockey clubs?

J: Sure. But assertive women are not necessarily sexually dominant. In fact they're often just the opposite in bed. There are ads in the personal columns. Or, you could state your wants to a friend—"I'd like you to call me and take charge of our next date." In a sexual setting you could say, "I've made love to you, now it's your turn to make love to me," or, "I want to play the shy virgin and have you seduce me, Are you willing?" Some women are just waiting for an invitation like that. Remember, women have grown up with the other side of your myth—men must always act, women must always react—and they might be feeling just as stuck in that role as you are in yours.

C: Do you think I could tell that woman in my Lit class what I was thinking after she walked out?

J: Do *you* think you could?

C: But she did say she wasn't into S & M.

J: Labels fit or don't fit wherever you stick them.

C: Yeah.

J: You might want to call me back and let me know how it goes. No, let me put it this way. . . What's your first name?

C: Nick.

J: Nick, I want you to phone me back next Thursday and tell me about your next interaction with that woman. In fact, I insist that you do. This is James, your master, speaking.

J: Yes, sir. (Laughter) Thanks for talking with me, James.

"You do that well, James. Do you think you could top Sam?" Pauli asked him when he got off the phone.

James seemed to consider the question seriously. "I might," he paused, "at least wilt his moustache."

"You've got the muscle, James, brute force," I said, "but Sam would probably lash you with his nasty tongue."

"Oh?" James put hands on his hips and stared at me meaningfully, a big man meaning big business.

"That doesn't sound half bad to me," Pauli smirked.

"A tongue lashing! That's not sexual," I protested. "It means a scolding, dressing down."

"Well, yes, that's a good part of it too," James barely smiled. "But it takes a really good man to get my boots off."

"Enough already. I give up. I'm going to hide out for a while with some uplifting literature." I grabbed the first magazine that came to hand and ducked my head behind it. Pauli's cackle made me check to see just exactly what I had grabbed. An ample blonde wearing a tightly-laced Victorian corset decorated the gaudy cover. Her large breasts, molded and emphasized by the garment, practically blocked her nostrils. "Well, you can certainly see how uplifting this is," I shrugged.

Stella was still giggling when she picked up the ringing phone.

Win The Battle, Lose The War

Stella: Sex Information.

Caller: I want to speak to a Lesbian.

S: There are none here right now. Can I help?

C: What are you?

S: Heterosexual, maybe bi.

C: Oh. One of those. I might have known.

S: Those?

C: Another straight woman who occasionally messes with her sisters then goes back into the straight world feeling politically correct because she's eaten a pussy.

S: Is that how you see bisexual women?

C: I don't see them. There is no such thing. You're either with us or against us.

S: I don't see sexual orientation as a war. I am an individual woman who relates primarily to men sexually. I have affectionate friendships with women and sometimes I'm sexual with them. But I'm not going to defend the label of heterosexual or bisexual. I don't have much energy around labels. Is there something else you wanted to talk about?

C: I want to talk with a Lesbian. When does one come on duty?

S: I really don't know who is what on the other shifts. You might try about six o'clock tonight, but maybe I can help in the meantime. I do know women's resources here in the city—clinics, bars, social organizations. I am well acquainted with women's bodies and how they function. And if it's a relationship concern, well, they're rarely gender-specific.

C: The hell you say.

S: You sound so angry. Won't you try talking with me?

C: No, not with you, traitor. I'll call back when there's a sister there!

The line went dead and Stella sighed.
"You can't win them all, kiddo," Pauli philosophized.
"That kind of generalized anger makes me so sad," Stella mourned. "You're with us or you're against us. The battle between the sexes is bad enough, but factions within the

sexes! You'd think militant Lesbians would have *some* feelings of identification with bisexual women. Consorting with the enemy, really!"

"Consorting with the enemy. . . ," Pauli turned to Stella. "I know you and Chile have been getting together, Star. Are you getting a similar kind of shit dumped on you?"

Stella stared at her. "Actually that hasn't even come up with me and Chile. If we have any problem it's about our conflicting schedules; we're both so busy. He's a man and I'm a woman, he's black and I'm white, he lives in the city and I live out in the Hills, and neither of us has a car. Those are the facts. Like I told that woman, relationship concerns are rarely gender-specific. I had the same time problem with a female lover two years ago. In our case, so far, race is as irrelevant as gender. We're just two people trying to find a way to be together, getting as much good stuff and as little grief as possible."

"Amen to that," James added.

"Sounds like that resonates with you, James, as they say. Do you have something in the works?" I smiled at him and hoped so.

"The lasso's in the air," he admitted.

"If you rope him, do you get two ears and a tail?" I asked.

"A piece of tail at least, one would hope." Pauli poked him and winked lewdly.

James grinned in appreciation, and I answered the next call.

They Say

Caller: I'm sixteen, and my girlfriends say I'm probably the last remaining virgin in my high school.

Isadora: You're saying you are sure you're the only sixteen year old who hasn't had intercourse?

C: I'm beginning to think so. All my friends have. One of them has been doing it with her boyfriend since she was fourteen. I know all the guys have done it.

I: You're sure about that?

C: They say so.

I: Well, that may be so. Boys *say* a lot of things they wish were true, or that they think other people expect to be true. Sometimes girls do too.

C: Why would a girl lie?

I: You tell me.

C: Well, there might be a few ugly ones who couldn't get anyone to have sex with them. Y'know, at least four girls in my class left school pregnant last year.

I: *They* were having intercourse for sure, then, weren't they? What about you, how do you feel about that? Do you have a boyfriend?

C: Yes.

I: Is he pressuring you to have intercourse with him?

C: Not really. He's had sex with other girls, though. He says he doesn't want me to do anything I don't want to do.

I: He sounds very understanding and mature.

C: Well, it's not as if I'm an Ice Princess. We make out, and I get him off with my hand.

I: Is that okay with you?

C: I guess so. But my friends say that's not going to keep him interested for very long.

I: Your friends are saying that to hold on to your boyfriend you should have intercourse?

C: Yes, that he won't be satisfied with this "kid stuff" for long. Is there something else we could do? I mean other than go all the way. I just don't think I'm ready for that yet, and I don't want to lose him.

I: Yes, there are other ways of being sexual together, and I'll get to that in a minute. But first, I want to get back to the idea that a girl can only keep her boyfriend by giving him sex. I just hate the idea of sex being used like a trading card—you buy my ticket to the movies and I'll put out five dollars worth of sex. That's demeaning to both people.

C: I pay my own way to the movies.

I: Great. So you get to pay your own way to the movies and you get to give him a hand job. Do you do that because you enjoy it or because you figure you owe it to him for some reason? What are *you* getting out of the relationship?

C: Well, I get to have a boyfriend, for now anyway.

I: Is it worth it? Do your friends who have intercourse all have the same boyfriends they started out with? Did *they* keep them by going all the way.

C: Not all of them.

I: Sometimes that doesn't work then, does it? And then where does it leave you?

C: Feeling used, I guess.

I: Used it is. That's not only a feeling, but a fact. Sex is something people share to give each other pleasure. If only one person gets any pleasure out of it, the other person can feel pretty bad. Is the social status of having a boyfriend worth the eventual pain of feeling used? Is it to you?

C: I don't know.

I: Do your girlfriends enjoy the sexual part of their relationships? Do they like intercourse?

C: One of them says she likes keeping her guy happy.

I: But you seem to be doing that, and you aren't running the risk of getting pregnant, or getting V.D., or feeling used. Isn't that so?

C: I guess so.

I: Look, I know you did not call to be given a lecture on what's wrong between the sexes. I guess I tend to do that sometimes. When I was growing up, young people did exactly the same things together that they always have. But they didn't talk about it. The myth then was that boys wanted all the sex they could get and the girl's job, if she was a "nice" girl, was to keep them from getting *any*. Boys insisted, girls resisted. So it went, push and pull.

C: It's still that way.

I: I liked keeping my boyfriend happy too. I also liked being touched and held and kissed. But none of my girlfriends admitted that they liked it, or that they even *did* it. I thought I was the only girl my age who had sexual feelings and that there was something wrong with me for not wanting to fight off my boyfriend's wandering hands.

C: Oh, yeah?

I: And now, twenty-five years later, here you are getting the opposite side of the myth — not that nice girls never enjoy sex, but that *everybody* is doing it and there is something wrong with you if you *don't* want to. You said earlier that you just don't feel ready to go all the way, to have intercourse.

C: I'm not.

I: Good. Listen to your feelings. You're lucky not to have the additional pressure from your boyfriend too, insisting that everybody is doing it. You said you get him off with your hand. Does he do that for you too?

C: I don't want him to touch me down there. It makes me feel. . . funny.

I: If you don't want him to, that's fine. If it feels "funny" because you think there's something unattractive about your sexual organs you might want to think about why you feel that way. Or, if the funny feeling is sexual excitement, and you find that scary, we could talk about that.

C: I just don't like it.

I: Okay. There was something else you wanted to talk about, wasn't there?

C: Yes, about what else I could do to keep him happy. One of my girlfriends said I could give him a blow job. But I was too embarrassed to ask her what she meant.

I: That's a slang term for having oral sex, kissing or caressing his penis with your mouth.

C: That's disgusting!

I: If you feel that way, then don't do it. Many people who feel close like to kiss each other all over. If a person is clean, there is no reason why any one part is okay to kiss and another part isn't. Since our genitals are often our most sensitive part, being kissed there is usually very exciting.

C: I don't want to do that.

I: That's very clear. It seems that you and your boyfriend are getting along just fine. What you're doing and not doing sexually is okay with you and it seems to be okay with him, too.

C: Yeah, it is.

I: If it's not okay with your girlfriends, well, they're not there when the two of you are alone. If they say you should do this or should try that, just tell them you don't want to, like you told me.

C: But what if my boyfriend starts asking for more?

I: Tell him the same thing, "I don't want to." It's your body, your feelings, your relationship. I admire your directness and other people will too. You just continue to do what you feel is right for you, okay? You're doing fine.

C: Yes. Thanks a lot.

When the call ended I found James and Stella chatting in the kitchen. "Stella has agreed to assist me," James announced to Pauli and me. "So I'd like extend a formal invitation to the Thursday Afternoon Shift to come to dinner at my house when we're finished here next week. Can you come?"

"Can I ever," Pauli drawled.

"I'd love to, James," I agreed.

"Good. I'll phone Sam at home during the week. You have his number, Pauli?

"Do I ever!" Pauli was on a roll. James ignored her.

"Any special occasion?" I asked.

"Do we need one?" James parried, "See you all next week." Only Pauli and I were left to straighten up and open the door for three volunteers struggling in with delicatessen boxes for the evening shift.

The phone rang as Pauli was gathering her purse and jacket. Everyone else seemed busy in the bathroom or kitchen. Shrugging, Pauli put down her things and reached for the phone, waving goodbye to me with her free hand. I decided to stay and listen. Hearing Pauli's breezy style was almost always as entertaining as it was educational.

How Much Is Too Much?

Pauli: Sex Information.

Caller: How big should a penis be?

P: I don't know how to answer you. How big should it be for what? If you want to wrap it around your leg and tuck it into your sock to keep your leg warm, it should be about 36 inches long.

C: Come on.

P: The average penis is between three inches and six inches. They have been known to be as small as one and one-half inches and as large as fourteen inches.

C: Where do you measure from?

P: If you want to rack up numbers you can measure from just in front of the asshole forward to the tip when it's erect. . . Hello?

C: . . .

P: Hello?

C: Well, then I'm seven and one-half inches.

P: Okay.

C: Don't women like them big?

P: Now, do you want me to tell you that as soon as women hear you have seven and one-half inches they're going to come beating down your door? Or do you want me to tell you that size has nothing to do with what kind of lover you are, that it isn't the meat, it's the motion. Which do you want to hear.

C: Which is true?

P: Either, or both. You know how Prince Charming is often described as tall, dark and handsome? Did you ever see any men who were short, blond, or funny-looking find a lover?

C: Sure.

P: Okay, suppose the woman of your dreams likes muscular blonds and you're a slender redhead?

C: Huh?. . . Uh, I could work out at the gym, and I guess I could dye my hair.

P: What if she likes men who are about five feet eight inches and you are six feet three inches? What are you gonna do? Cut yourself off at the ankles? Whether a woman prefers five-inch penises or nine-inch ones, you have seven and one-half inches. What can you do about it?

C: Nothing, I guess.

P: Well, there you are. You've got what you've got. Yes, there are some women who prefer big penises, or thick ones, or circumsized ones. Just as there are people who really go for blue-eyed baldies. If you've got what she wants, great. If you don't, she may reject you if your penis isn't perfectly to her liking. On the other hand, you might win her over with your flashing smile and charming ways, even if you're cross-eyed and hung like a canary.

C: Yes, but isn't it usually better to be bigger?

P: For some people. Actually, I've heard more women mention the thickness or slenderness of a penis than I have the length.

C: How thick should it be?

P: (Sighing) I don't know. I know very few people who consider or reject a potential sexual partner with a tape measure. There are some people who will only have sex with partners who meet very particular requirements; like being rich, the same religion, etc. You either have it or you don't. You can get it or you can't. I've spoken to men who felt their penis was so large that potential partners took off as soon as they took off their pants. It's all in how you look at it, you, and the person you want to have sex with.

C: You mentioned circumsized cocks. Do women prefer them cut or uncut?

P: If I say cut, and you are not, are you going to run out and get circumsized today?

C: Hell, no.

P: Then what's the point? There is no answer to that anyway. Some people prefer circumsized penises, some un-. Some people have very strong feelings on the matter, some couldn't care less. If you have more than one sexual partner throughout your life, you will probably run into both. Does your penis work?

C: It works fine.

P: Good. Then it's exactly the right size for you.

7

THE DINNER PARTY

The following week was slow at the Switchboard, and after phoning to check the action, both James and Pauli decided not to come in. Both of them at home "cooking," as Sam said, as their respective talents dictated. I liked his turn of phrase. Stella lay on the floor doing stretching exercises, and left after an hour to help James prepare the dinner. Sam leafed through a Scandinavian porn magazine, occasionally chuckling. I turned the pages of a beautifully photographed book about men making love to themselves. *Chacun à son goût.* The phones were silent for almost thirty minutes at a time.

The shift was notable only in that I completed what I felt was my briefest total phone transaction.

Caller: What does a pussy taste like?

Isadora: What does a pussy taste like? Well. . . can you tell me what strawberry jam tastes like?

C: I don't know how to describe a taste.

I: Well, neither do I.

Sam looked up at me from his magazine, "It doesn't taste like strawberry jam." I shook my head, "Gee, I'd always hoped it did."

By 5:45 we had answered no more than three "What's a . . . ?" calls, and maybe one or two "How do you . . . ?" inquiries apiece. I commented that I thought I could describe how to fuck in my sleep. To which Sam's laconic response was, "Sounds like my first wife." We left together when Helen, the evening shift supervisor, arrived carrying a pineapple.

"Don't they do anything but eat from six to nine?" Sam asked."Not to worry. James will see that we're well fed tonight, I'm sure. If dinner consists of nothing but one of his cakes, I'll be satisfied."

"You're obviously easy to satisfy," Sam jibed. When I seemed oblivious to his dig, he went on smoothly, "I require a more varied meal."

James's apartment was in a modern stucco apartment building in the Avenues. Pauli was seated on a large squooshy gray couch drinking wine when Sam and I came in. James, wearing a black vinyl apron bearing the logo "It isn't pretty being easy," and brandishing a wire whisk, let us in and trotted back into the kitchen muttering, "Timing is everything." Stella came out of the kitchen carrying two filled wine glasses. Her long red hair was unbraided in celebration of the occasion of our coming together off duty. The silky fall of hair covering her back rippled as she walked.

"Stella, you look so lovely." I smiled at her, feeling quite maternal.

"That should rightfully be my line, woman." Sam took a glass from Stella's hand and gently touched a strand of hair which floated across her shoulder. "You must wear it loose more often. It's very becoming."

"Thank you both," Stella said simply. "I accept compliments from both sexes."

"That's Stella all right—bisuggestional," James called from the next room. We all groaned.

Pauli raised her glass in a salute, "I wish I'd said that."

"You will," Sam smirked.

Chile arrived in due time, carrying a bouquet of white roses which he ceremoniously presented to James along with a backthumping hug. Stella's glow heightened when he followed with a hug for her. The rest of us were on our second bottle of Green Hungarian wine. A large platter of crab and cheese puffs was only a happy memory.

We were all laughing at one of Sam's dry "tales of the classroom" stories when James announced dinner.

In a small room off the kitchen was a picture-perfect, elegantly laid, round table—crimson cloth to the floor, crisp white place mats, two cut crystal glasses to the right of each banded china plate, and enough heavy silver cutlery at each place to discomfit all but the most socially secure. There were ornately carved individual salt dishes, and a set of heavy silver candlesticks with red tapers ablaze. It was, to say the least, awe-inspiring.

"I promise never to envy the evening shift their burnt casseroles again. M'god, James," Pauli said, "I always thought of bachelor dinners as canned spaghetti on paper plates, fresh spaghetti on plastic plates if the guy is a real gourmet."

James seated us all with great ceremony, carefully arranging the fall of Stella's hair over her chair back, deftly whisking linen napkins from their swanlike folds onto each awaiting lap. After seating himself, he lifted a small silver hand bell to his left and tinkled it. "You may serve now, Galt."

Five heads turned toward the door and five mouths fell simultaneously agape as the first course was presented—a silver tray of individual cups of sour cream-topped cucumber soup, each in its own ice-packed silver liner. Impressive enough, it was not *what* was presented but *how* that was causing the collective goggle. The silver tray was silently handed around by a slender blond young man who was nude except for a starched white apron, a black and white frilly French maid's cap perched atop his curls, and pancake makeup, which did not quite cover his post-(I hoped) adolescent acne.

Other than murmured thank-yous as each person was served, no words were spoken. The silence continued after our server left the room, broken only by discrete slurps and the ting of silver spoons against crystal cups. Dish after dazzling dish followed—a seafood mousse, tidbits of marinated pork on bronze skewers, tiny dilled carrots, a rice pilaf filled with sweet and crunchy unidentifiables, and a tart lime sorbet with the subtle aroma of rum. Everything was delicate, surprising, exquisitely prepared, and served and eaten in silence. Sporadic exclamations ("Fantastic soup!") or attempts at conversation ("I've never tasted rice prepared that way") were silenced as soon as our serving person arrived to pass a dish or clear one. Then all eyes would lower and silence would descend again.

Putting down his spoon beside the empty sorbet dish, James arose and returned with a lacquered box containing slender dark brown cigarillos which he offered to all. Only Stella declined. "We'll have coffee shortly," James pronounced. This occasioned a clatter of busyness in the kitchen. He leaned back and puffed his cigar with a sigh of satisfaction, then looked around the table with the smile of a generous host. I'd never seen James smoke before. In fact, I'd never seen anything like this dinner before. "I guess you're waiting for an explanation for all this." He flipped his large hand around the room and toward the kitchen, in an uncharacteristic gesture of expansiveness.

"James you don't have to. . . " Stella spoke softly.

"Oh shut up, Star," Pauli interrupted. "Yes he does. You didn't get *that* help from the State Employment Service. C'mon, James. Tell."

"Galt, will you come here please?" James barely raised his voice and the young man appeared in the doorway.

"Yes, sir?"

"Will you tell my friends what you're doing here, please."

Galt grinned briefly and showed a flash of unexpected dimples. "I'm his birthday present," he explained.

"Is it your birthday?" "Oh, James." "Hot damn!" We all spoke up at once. James stopped us by continuing to address Galt. "And am I mistreating you in any way?"

"Oh no, sir. Not yet anyway. But I do have hopes for after your friends leave." He dimpled again, and Sam laughed aloud.

James's mouth twitched but he spoke solemnly. "That will be all, Galt. We'll be ready for coffee in a few minutes."

The young man left the room, and we all began to laugh and talk at the same time as if recess had been declared.

"Oh, James. Happy, happy birthday," Stella said.

"Damn, James. That sure beats flowers." Chile slapped his thigh in delight.

"I didn't think anything could faze me, James, but I was plussed and nonplussed, I tell you." Sam shook his head in admiration.

"My birthday's in October," Pauli said. "Does he do windows?"

"Who gave him to you?" I asked.

"He did," James answered. "He's an orderly at the hospital. We've been talking a lot over the past months. Weeks ago he asked me the standard California question about my birth sign and about ten days ago he gave me a scroll which said that a slave would arrive at 8 AM on my birthday morning and be mine to do with what I wanted for twenty-four hours. So I decided to give myself this birthday dinner."

"I know what he was doing for the past twelve hours anyway," I said.

"You do, do you?" James looked at me quizzically.

"Polishing silver!" I held up one of the three pieces still left at my setting. "This is really breathtaking, James. Did you inherit it from a titled ancestor?"

"No, I've been buying silver at auctions over the years. I knew someday I'd get out of Wyoming and into big city living. I'm proud of each piece, I think it beats collecting stamps for an investment. I love it when I get a chance to use it like tonight."

"Hurrah for you," shouted Pauli. "Shall we leave right after coffee so you can find something else creative to do with your slave?"

"No hurry," James said. "He still has to do the dishes."

"Before he gets to do the host," Chile piped up.

"James," Pauli said, "you're not doing as well as Cinderella. She didn't have twenty-four hours and look what she accomplished."

I asked in a low voice, "Is Galt the dogie you were rustling, or however your cowboy lingo goes?"

"I had my hopes," James said modestly. Galt entered carrying a souffle on top of which was a Fourth of July sparkler spitting dazzles. He led us all in a rousing round of Happy Birthday and returned to the kitchen.

"That was not part of your orders, boy," James called out.

In response, part of Galt re-entered the doorway, the rear part, which wiggled saucily and disappeared back into the kitchen to a chorus of hoots and giggles.

"The service around here is really deteriorating." James shook his head. "The help must be getting into the cooking sherry."

The soufflé itself was liberally laced with Grand Marnier. I had paid almost five dollars for a piece of one that couldn't touch it at one of the city's best restaurants. Those who drank the coffee praised it lavishly. Sam and James had a brief debate over the merits of various filtering devices.

"That was truly a superb meal, James. I am extremely impressed." Murmurs of assent seconded me from all sides. "I once said you were a man of many surprises."

"And you hadn't seen nothin' yet," James rumbled his amusement.

"You're absolutely right. I sit abashed, only because I'm too stuffed to stand right now," Sam responded.

"Speaking of surprises. . . ," Pauli broke in.

"And getting stuffed. . . ," Stella hiccoughed.

"No more wine for her, folks." Pauli gave Stella a mock frown. "I have a surprise to announce."

"You're pregnant?"

"You're going to have a sex change operation?"

"You're getting married?"

"Now that's really kinky," Pauli said to the last suggestion.

"I'm going to be interviewed on TV in the next few weeks. Channel 9 is doing a documentary on new therapy modes, and surrogates are finally beginning to be recognized as something different than sex for money."

"New therapy modes? Oh god," Sam moaned, "you're going to be sandwiched between a spaced-out guru into primal whimpers and a robot computer programmed to recite 'Would you care to say more about that?'"

"Probably worse," Pauli laughed, "But who gives a shit.

It's good legitimate publicity and I plan to dazzle them with my lady-like professionalism."

"Or baffle 'em with your bullshit," Chile said.

"Be sure to wear a bra," I suggested.

"Hell, If Pauli even owns panties. . . ," Sam said.

". . . you'd eat them," Pauli finished.

"What do you plan to say, Pauli?" Stella asked. "What do you feel is most important about the work you do?"

"I think people need to know that sexual surrogates can be a legitimate complement to conventional therapies, and in a few cases, an excellent substitute. We are an important resource for people with little or no sexual experience, or for those learning to live with a physical disability. A surrogate can fix some of those problems as easily as a tennis pro can correct a faulty serve, and it needn't be any more embarrassing than taking tennis lessons."

"Minus the fuzzy balls. That's a heavy banner for you to wave, Pauli my dear," Sam smirked. "Do you think the world is ready?"

Peter on the Training Staff does sexual surrogate work too, doesn't he?" Stella asked.

"Yes. I've suggested they have him on the show too. Then I won't have to wave my heavy banner alone." She made a face at Sam. "The taping will be some time next week. It's not all together yet. I'll keep you guys posted."

Galt came into the room and silently settled on the floor at James's feet. James stroked his curls with absentminded affection, and occasionally puffed on his small brown cigar. Stella and Chile sat close together on the couch, their fingers entwined. Sam continued the exchange with Pauli, baiting her and getting as good as he gave. Vivaldi was playing softly in the background. I looked around at this odd assortment of faces, leaned back and felt full—in body, mind and heart.

MOVING ON

Sam was on the phone.

But We Need The Eggs

Caller: I have a question. It isn't about sex, but may I ask it anyway?

Sam: I'm a whiz at spelling and I can tell you the plot of most operas. Go ahead and try me.

C: It's about relationships.

S: It generally is.

C: Well, since you're a man maybe you can answer this. How can I get a man to make and keep a commitment?

S: Do you mean like to monogamy, fidelity?

C: No. I said this wasn't about sex, or not yet anyway.

S: Would you be more specific then? What sort of commitment?

C: Well, that word seems to be the dirty word of the ages. That, and Love. But I'm not getting to that yet either. I'm talking about. . . oh, things like, "I'll call you."

S: What you want to know is how to get someone to call you who says he is going to call you and then doesn't?

C: When you put it like that, it sounds ridiculous.

S: Isn't that what you said?

C: I guess so, but I'm not sure that's what I mean, or not entirely.

S: Okay, let's start again. What is it that you want?

C: What I *want* is a relationship.

S: Ah-ha.

C: And I guess what I want to know is what's wrong with men that they're so unwilling to make a commitment.

S: Wait. Back up. The first statement was very concise: "I want a relationship." Then you said, or implied, that because you don't have one, or one that's satisfactory to you, there is something wrong with men in general.

C: Well, with the ones I meet.

S: Ah-ha. That's different. Who are you trying to have relationships with, or with whom, to be precise?

C: Men.

S: Married men? Homosexual men? Men under twenty? Don Juans? What sort of men are you attracted to?

C: I'm twenty-nine years old and I haven't had one single relationship that's lasted more than five or six months.

S: Yes?

C: Well?

S: Those are relationships, aren't they? Even one night stands are relationships of a kind. They have beginnings, middles and ends, even if they're unsatisfactory.

C: What I want is a man in my life who loves me, who I can depend on, and have some sort of future with. Not necessarily marriage, but I want that to be a possibility.

S: Good. All right. And are you meeting men like that?

C: I don't think men like that exist any more. They say they'll call and they don't. They say they're interested, but they just drift away, or they say they don't want to get involved, or things are getting too "heavy." You know, no commitment. It's a dirty word.

S: Whoa. Back up. "They say, they do." You're back into indicting the whole sex again. Is it fair to say that the men in your life so far don't seem to be looking for the same things you're looking for?

C: Yes, but . . .

S: Wait. Is that a fair assessment so far?

C: Yes.

S: All right. If that's true, there are several possible reasons why. One, you're barking up the wrong trees, so to speak. You're looking for something from men who are looking for different things, have different goals. Men do get married all the time, in the hundreds of thousands, or live with their lovers, or have passionate affairs that last years.

C: Not with me they don't.

S: We get more calls here from men who are looking for Ms. Right than we do from women. The second possibility is that you're not communicating effectively with the men you meet. Somewhere the wires originating from you are getting crossed.

C: You're saying that no matter what, it's my fault, not the men's.

S: Whoa . . .

C: I'm disgusted. If it's not working, then it's *my* fault. I'm too unclear, or too pushy, or asking too much. I'm too something, anyway. You men are all alike.

S: Wait. Can you put aside your indignation for just one minute and play a game. Let's pretend that I'm a man you've gone out with. It looks like there might be some possibilities between us. We've ended our time together tonight with a juicy goodnight kiss or a great tumble in bed, whatever, and I say, "Thanks for a great evening. I'll call you later in the week." What happens now?

C: You probably won't call.

S: That's what you're thinking to yourself, but what would you say to me?

C: I'd probably say exactly that.

S: All right. If I was leaving the company of a woman I'd just spent some good time with and I said, "I'll call you," and she said to me, "You probably won't," I'd feel very defensive. My reaction would be, to put it bluntly, "Well, screw you, bitch. I *won't* call then." I might not say that but I'd think it *and* I wouldn't call.

C: See!

S: See what? What we've got here now is two angry people, each feeling abused. Who wants to commit to that?

C: Yes, but . . .

S: You were saying to a man you just kissed or made love with that you don't trust him to keep his promise. You may have had that experience often enough, but is it *my* fault that the other men in your life have been bastards? I'm a nice guy. I haven't done anything except have a good time with you, said so, stated my intentions of seeing you again, and I get hit with an accusation which I feel is unfair.

C: Well, I think it's unfair that you think it's *my* fault that I'm not getting what I want.

S: All right, let's set aside the blaming. What could you say to me when I say I'll call that isn't likely to make me feel defensive?

C: Um. . . "I hope you do. I enjoyed being with you."

S: That's great! I'd love to hear that. And I recognize that saying that might stick in your teeth if you're *feeling* like, "Oh yeah, I've heard that before." One thing you might do is take the ball into your own hands and say, "How's about if I call *you*, say, Thursday evening." That gives you control. It would keep you from sitting by the phone getting angrier or more depressed when he, I, don't call as soon as you think I should.

C: That sounds pushy to me.

S: Then what about saying exactly what's on you mind; no accusations, just a simple statement of fact: "When someone says 'I'll call you' to me I immediately think, 'Oh, yeah, sure, the social lie.' If you would like to get together again, and Iwould, can we make a date now?" Or, you might say, "May I suggest that if you're going to call, Tuesday afternoon would be a good time to reach me."

C: Isn't that pushy too?

S: I'd call it being assertive. I'd rather hear that, I assure you than, "You probably won't call." What I hear is that you want to see me again too, which I like, and that you're willing to take some responsibility for moving things along by either calling me or telling me exactly when I can reach you.

C: Does it really make that much difference what I say or how I say it? You're either going to call or not call, regardless.

S: Don't you have any control in this?

C: Not much, if any.

S: If you feel that way, no wonder you're angry. I'd be angry too if I wasn't getting what I wanted and felt there wasn't anything I could do about it. You're blaming men as a sex, and you feel that I'm blaming you as a person. I'm saying look at what's happening and what you can do to increase yoI can reach you.

C: Does it really make that much difference what I say or how I say it? You're either going to call or not call, regardless.

S: Don't you have any control in this?

C: Not much, if any.

S: If you feel that way, no wonder you're angry. I'd be angry too if I wasn't getting what I wanted and felt there wasn't anything I could do about it. You're blaming men as a sex, and you feel that I'm blaming you as a person. I'm saying look at what's happening and what you can do to increase your chances of making it different, better. I'm suggesting that you make clear what you want, in such a way that I'm not likely to get defensive or angry. "I would like you to phone me Tuesday," sounds a great deal more to the point, unmuddied, than, "You say you will but probably won't and a pox on you and your whole gender."

C: (Sigh) Maybe you're right. But I get so angry, so depressed at the endless. . . bullshit I have to go through.

S: Me too. I could give you a very long list of my own complaints about your sex. For example, when I ask a woman out for a certain night, and she says she's busy, does that mean,"I'm busy that night *and* I'd like you to ask me for another night?" Or does it mean, "I plan to be busy for the rest of my life whenever *you* call, you jerk!" If I call again and she meant the latter, I'm being pushy, insensitive, and laying my ego on the line for another severe bruising. If she simply meant she was busy that particular night, and I don't call her again because I don't want to be rejected again, she assumes I'm not interested, and a possible great relationship shrivels on the vine.

C: She could call you.

S: She *could*. So could you phone those men who don't call you back, but do you? Who *likes* being rejected?

C: It seems a wonder that men and women get together at all.

S: Some great sage once said that relationships are like chickens. They're dirty, messy, troublesome. . . but we need the eggs.

C: (Laughing) Yeah, chicken shit and all. . . You sound like a very nice man. Would you like to get together with me?

S: I probably would, dear lady, if for no other reason than to restore the honor of my sex in your eyes. And I do thank you for extending the invitation; it cannot have been easy for you. But we here at the Switchboard are not permitted to meet callers in person. We agree to that when we volunteer, and I, and all the other volunteers, male and female, keep our commitments.

C: Okay. Anyway, it's nice to know that there are men in the world willing to make some kind of commitment.

S: We're out here, I assure you.

C: Do you hold your meetings in a telephone booth? Listen. I would like to call you again sometime. May I?

S: Dear lady, I don't know your name and I'm not asking it for obvious reasons, but that was magnificently clear communication and I appreciate it mightily. My name is Sam. You can reach me here Thursday afternoons from three until six, but only until the end of the month. I'm leaving the area in September for greener pastures. Somewhere out there is a fine sensitive woman who will heal my battle scars from the relationship wars of the past, and to whom I can offer the same.

C: I really hope you find her.

S: And I hope you find him. May Eros bless us both on our search.

C: Well, goodbye for now. Maybe somewhere our paths will cross.

As soon as Sam was off the phone I bent over and kissed the top of his thinning hair. I was touched almost to tears by his honesty. "Awww, Sam, that was so nice. For a man who can be so abrasive, you are astonishingly sensitive at times."

"You make me sound like some sort of human emery board," Sam blustered, embarrassed at being overheard and confronted in such a personal conversation.

"Did I hear you say you were going away, Sam?" Stella asked.

"Yes, and James, I do not want any sort of obscene Going

Away cake. I shall simply fold my tent and silently steal away on the first of September. No fuss, no muss."

"Pauli tells me you've been here for years," James said. "Can't we mark the occasion of your leaving in some meaningful way?"

"Well," Sam paused to ponder as he stroked his moustache, "You might think of having a game of goodbye grab-ass with me, Isadora, a bon voyage bang, a frolic of farewell fornication." Ah, here he was again, back to his old tricks.

"As your last caller would say, Sam, 'You men are all the same.' I wouldn't say that, of course," I said.

"What are your plans? Where are you going?" Stella asked. The phone intruded. "Darn. I'll get that call. Don't answer until I'm finished." She picked up the receiver.

Get Me To A Nunnery

Stella: Sex Information. Can I help you?

Caller: Is there any reason a woman might miss her period?

S: Any reason other than the obvious one? Have you missed yours?

C: I'm two weeks late.

S: Could you be pregnant?

C: Oh God, I hope not.

S: It's not too soon to have a pregnancy test.

C: Do I have to give my name if I do? Oh god, my mother would kill me. I just can't be pregnant. What would I do?

S: May I ask how old you are?

C: I'm eighteen. I don't want a baby. I'm not ready to get married. Oh god, if I get through this I'm going to become a nun.

S: Please calm down. I guess there is a reason for you to think you might be pregnant.

C: We didn't even go all the way. He only put a little of it inside me. Oh, I told him we shouldn't. What will I do?

S: The first thing is to find out if you *are* pregnant. First of all, where are you calling from?

C: Why?

S: If I know, I can give you the phone number of a women's clinic near you, or Planned Parenthood. You can have a confidential pregnancy test. And if you're not pregnant, they can tell you about birth control so that you won't have to go through this every month.

C: Are you kidding? I'm never going to go near my boyfriend again. I told you, I'll become a nun. But what if I am. . . pregnant? What can I do?

S: If you are, you have several options. It's not the end of the world. There are counselors at the clinics to help you make a decision that's right for you.

C: Like what?

S: Well, if keeping the baby is out of the question, you might consider having it and giving it up for adoption. There are various facilities that would help you. Or you might want to consider an abortion.

C: On my god!

S: Look, none of the options is pleasant, but you don't have to enter a convent. Not knowing is awful, so don't wait. The problem won't go away by itself. Get a test this week. If you wait too long, you won't be able to have an abortion even if you decide that's what you want to do.

C: What should I do? I don't want anyone to know.

S: Call the clinic and make an appointment. They might ask you to bring in a urine sample, or they might take a bit of blood from your finger. Nothing major. You can get the test results in less than 48 hours, sometimes even immediately. If you're not pregnant, you can relax and do whatever you need to do so this won't happen again. If you are, you can make an immediate appointment with a counselor to go over your options.

C: Uh. . . tell me about abortions. How would I get one? I don't have much money.

S: Abortion is only one option. If you decide that's what you need to do, the clinic will refer you or do it there within a week or so. At this time in our state, they won't need to tell your parents, and some clinics work on a sliding fee scale. For several weeks into the pregnancy, say within the first three or four months, the method used most often is aspiration.

C: What's that?

S: It's sort of like a small vacuum cleaner which is used to suck out the contents of the uterus through the vagina. It's relatively uncomplicated and painless. After the first few months of pregnancy, an abortion gets more complicated.

C: Oh.

S: The aspiration method is a possibility sometimes, but the other method used is a saline injection into the uterus which actually causes labor. What you are doing is passing a fetus as if you were giving birth.

C: That sounds horrible.

S: But many hospitals and clinics refuse to do abortions at all after a certain point, because it's dangerous to the woman, and because the fetus has the potential of being born alive.

C: Oh my god.

S: May I ask your first name?

C: (Crying) It's. . . Laura. Oh, what'll I do?

S: Laura, my name is Star. Please listen to me. Call the number I'll give you and make an appointment. Call me back next week at this time and tell me what happened. We will know more then. You might be late simply because you are so upset. Okay? Will you make the call if I give you the number?

C: I'm afraid to find out that I am, Star.

S: It won't go away by itself. If you want to talk to someone before next week, you can call here any time between three and nine o'clock during the week. But please get a pregnancy test right away . . . Laura?

C: Isn't there some sort of test I can take at home?

S: There are home pregnancy tests, but you can't really count on them. If the results are negative, it might only mean that it's too soon to tell. If it's positive, any doctor you go to will want to give you another test anyway. Save yourself ten dollars and go get it done at a clinic. Is it the clinic setting that bothers you?

C: I think. . . I'd rather go to somebody I know. . . like my own doctor.

S: Do you trust your doctor to keep your confidence if you decide not to tell your parents?

C: I don't know.

S: Can you call your doctor and ask?

C: Ask what?

S: Say something like, "I want to see you in confidence. Will you do that, or will you tell my parents?" Then if you feel your doctor is trustworthy, by all means go, if it will make it easier. Just get a reliable test as soon as possible. And Laura, please call me back and let me know.

C: Okay.

S: Good luck. I'll be rooting for you.

"My youngest daughter is named Laura," Sam said pensively.

"Poor thing was so panicked," Stella frowned in sympathy. "I wish I could take her to a clinic myself."

"It gets harder staying uninvolved, not easier, I think," Sam said. "I'm really looking forward to getting away from all these problems. Soon, my biggest dilemma will be whether to have my beer in a glass or out of the bottle."

"Where are you going, Sam?" Stella asked again.

"I'm on sabbatical from the college. I've sublet my condo

for a year. First of all I'm going to visit my oldest daughter in Santa Fe for two or three weeks. Beyond that I have no plans. I'll travel, maybe fall in love with some place or someone. I'm so tired of students' problems, callers' problems, my own problems."

"And of course if you fall in love there will be no problems, right?" I teased. I wanted to tread gently.

Sam laughed. "I suppose I'm just ready for different ones in a different setting."

"Have you considered being gay?" James asked. "That would be new and different."

"No, James. Is that an invitation?" Sam asked, smiling slightly.

"Would you like it to be?" James asked, not smiling at all.

One beat, two. Sam lowered his eyes. "No, I don't think so."

"Good, then it wasn't meant that way. Consider it merely a suggestion of alternatives." James winked impishly at me, and reached for the ringing phone. So he *could* top Sam! Another phone rang within seconds, and I picked it up.

Strangers In The Night

Isadora: Sex Information. May I help you?

Caller: Oh good, a woman. May I ask you, are you married?

I: I have been.

C: Oh. Well. . . I am a married woman.

I: Yes?

C: I mean I am *married*. None of these almost or open-style arrangements. I married my husband "for better or for worse, keeping myself only unto him until death do us part." I believe in keeping the marriage vows.

I: Yes.

C: I was a virgin when I married him and I have no regrets. But, lately. . . I've been having these thoughts. . . When I. . . Oh, this is impossibly embarrassing.

I: I'm listening. Take your time.

C: The physical part of my husband's love for me and mine for him is very satisfactory. He is a good father to our children, and we share a lot of interests. In every way I am a happily married woman.

I: Yes.

C: Well, lately I've been having these thoughts, fantasies, I guess you'd call them, about. . . about making love with another man.

I: You've been having fantasies about making love with some other man.

C: Not any particular other man. That's what's so disturbing to me. I can certainly understand finding another man of my acquaintance attractive. That's happened occasionally. I might think about what it might have been like if I had married someone other than my husband, what it might be like being held or kissed by this man or that. It's a pleasant reverie and doesn't hurt anyone. But these thoughts lately aren't about anyone in particular. It's. . . I. . . When my husband and I are making love, if I close my eyes and pretend that he's a stranger, a big black man with an Afro haircut, lots of muscles, and an enormous. . . organ, well, I get very aroused.

I: Umm.

C: It's arousing, and extremely disturbing to me. I love my husband.

I: And you find it disturbing that you have fantasies about another man, or other men, when you are together sexualy.

C: Yes. And that it is a black man bothers me. I'm not a bigot. We have black men and women in our circle of acquaintances. I'm aware of the myth that black people are more savage, more sexually knowledgable than white people, and that black men are reputed to have larger sexual organs. . .

I: You know that these are fantasies, then.

C: Yes. People are people on an individual basis. What also bothers me about my. . . thoughts is that the stranger who is making love to me in my imagination, does so. . . roughly. My husband is a gentle man, a gentle sexual partner. It's one of the qualities I most appreciate about him. He wouldn't think of being brutal, mentally or physically, and I wouldn't like it if he was. What does it mean? I don't want to make love with anyone other than my husband. I don't want to be brutalized. I don't believe that I am attracted to any of the black men we know. . . yet, I must be, or why would I be thinking of it. I'm afraid that I might go out and do something unthinkable if I can't stop these dreadful fantasies.

I: I can see how upsetting it is to you.

C: Oh, it is.

I: First let me assure you that most people have fantasies. And they are just that—flights of fancy, not necessarily wishes. A healthy person can choose to act on a fantasy, or not to act on it.

C: You think these fantasies of mine are *healthy?*

I: They're not healthy for you if you find them so upsetting, but I assure you that're very common among women, even happily married ones. Have you ever read any books by Nancy Friday?

C: No.

I: There's one called *My Secret Garden* and another called *Forbidden Flowers*. They're both collections of women's sexual fantasies drawn from thousands that have been sent to her anonymously. If you read them you'll find some that will strike you as extremely bizarre, and others might seem familiar to you. Some you might find arousing in a way that doesn't disturb you as much as your own with the rough black stranger.

C: But are these from normal women?

I: I'm sure that most of the women who contributed them

were healthy functioning members of their community, sharing something as private as their fantasies so that women like yourself might feel better. Strangers, large penises, brutality, even rape are common themes in many perfectly healthy women's fantasies. No woman would actually *want* to be raped. But a woman might want to play with her fantasies, whatever they are.

C: What? Are you suggesting that I actually have sex with a black stranger or have my husband rape me?

I: Not at all. A person can choose not to act out his or her fantasies for any of several good reasons. One, as in your case, because it's against her personal ethics.

C: Yes.

I: Another reason might be that a favorite fantasy is impossible to fulfill such as, "I would like to grow a penis and make love to myself as if I were my own lover." . . . Or a person might refrain from acting out a fantasy because of the consequences, "I would like to make love to every man on my husband's softball team, one by one." A healthy person can make choices about her behavior.

C: Why a healthy person?

I: A few people feel compelled to act out fantasies regardless of the likely consequences, such as men who are sexually attracted to young children.

C: Ugh.

I: There are those whose fantasies twist their perceptions of reality such as flashers; you know, men who expose themselves in public places. I've spoken to two here at the Switchboard and each of them had hopes, fantasies, that when a woman saw his exposed penis she would become instantly aroused and have sex with him.

C: That's ridiculous. What did you say to them?

I: I said that most women react with fear, annoyance, disgust, amusement. . . any number of feelings, but that it was extremely unlikely that one would react with desire to an exhibition like that from a strange man.

C: Of course.

I: Both men admitted that women displayed all of the reactions I mentioned, that none had ever responded the way they hoped. Still, their fantasy is that one day someone will. The reality is that such a man will probably be arrested or disgraced long before that possibility. At the very least, he will remain unsatisfied.

C: Well?

I: You see, that's how a fantasy that is not identified as such can be distorted.

C: What do you tell someone with fantasies that are. . . antisocial, like child molesters or exhibitionists?

I: First I tell them what the consequences of their acts are under the law: probable arrest and imprisonment. Second, I might make some suggestions on how they can reconcile real life with their fantasy life.

C: Such as?

I: The man who likes children might seek very slender, youthful partners, above the legal age of consent, and ask them to dress or act in a certain way to heighten the fantasy effect. The flasher can learn some social skills in any number of classes and workshops which would help him make more effective connections.

C: What if being looked at is what he wants?

I: There are nudist clubs and beaches where he can parade to his hearts content—although I'd certainly caution him that there are strict rules about behavior in such places. Leaping out from behind bushes and "weenie wagging" is frowned on everywhere.

C: That's certainly interesting, but back to my problem. What should I do?

I: What would you like to do?

C: Well, nothing. I certainly don't want to be raped by a stranger. I don't want to be sexual with anyone other than my husband. I'm satisfied with the size of my husband's organ. Even if I weren't, there's not much either of us could do about that, is there? I enjoy my husband's gentle ways. . . most of the time.

I: That's a less definitive statement than you made before.

C: Well, I never thought of playing with fantasies before. Mine were so upsetting to me, not something to be taken lightly. But I see there are some possibilities here I might think about.

I: Would it be possible for your husband to comb his hair into an Afro?

C: (Laughing) Not very likely. Oh, I do thank you. I feel so much better after talking with someone about all this.

I: I'm delighted. Please do look into the books I mentioned. Maybe you'll discover a fantasy you like better. Feel free to phone again if you want to talk some more.

C: I will. Thank you again. Good bye.

"We seem to have had lots of calls from women today," James mentioned. "Why do you think that is?"

"Maybe it's the phase of the moon," Sam answered.

"Maybe it's because women are discovering that they have things to complain about, the right to ask questions, the need to take action," I started to declaim.

"Right on!" Stella cheered.

"Sexist sow," Sam taunted.

"Fight! Fight!" Stella started bouncing around and tossed the pillow she was sitting on in Sam's direction. "Come on, Isadora, the girls against the boys."

I approached James in mock combat stance. He stood up, and I found myself eye level with his third shirt button. No fool I, I hugged him around the waist instead. The hug was returned in kind.

"Do you know that poem by Shel Silverstein?" I asked, tilting my head up to him. "I think it goes:

I will not play at tug of war
I'd rather play at hug of war
Where everyone hugs instead of tugs
Where everyone giggles
And rolls on the rug.
Where everyone kisses
And everyone grins
And everyone cuddles
And everyone wins."

I leaned against his big comfortable belly for a moment and murmured into his chest, "Are things going well for you on the homefront, James?"

"Better than I ever dreamed of," he rumbled into my hair.

"I'm so glad," I smiled. "You deserve it."

"Don't we all? What did Sam say? May Eros bless us all on our search."

"Amen. . . or A-women." That was Stella.

9

THE STAR

"You are looking at a star, a goddamned star" Pauli sang out as she entered the room the following week.

"Pauli, how did it go? Was the show taped?" We crowded around her as she took off her coat.

"Taped last week, to be aired who knows when. But when it is, I expect to become a star. You may touch me," she waltzed grandly around James, "non-sexually, of course."

"Of course." James bowed. "And did m'lady remember to wear underwear for her debut?"

"You know, I really don't remember. But I was so demure that if I'd been on trial for doing in my parents, I would have had the judge offering mercy because I was an orphan. I really do think it went well. I was prepared for one of those smirky interviewer's questions, 'Now tell me Ms. Baker, how does what you do differ from being a. . . er. . . ahem. . . a prostitute, if I may ask?' I didn't get any of that shit. I was on a panel with a psychologist from L. A. who makes referrals to sexual surrogates regularly, and a woman physician who specializes in sexual dysfunctions. She began to see how useful surrogate work could be in her practice. Of course, the whole program might be shown at 6 A.M. on Labor Day. You know, in one of those public service slots. Then the only person who will see it will be a 79-year-old insomniac in East Cow Flop, Texas, but what the hell. It was fun doing it."

"Speaking about doing it. . . ," Pauli leered eagerly and I continued, "Shouldn't we get to work?" All four phones were lit up.

"Where's Old Faithful?" Pauli asked. She had just noticed Sam's absence.

"Sam? He's probably getting ready to leave," Stella answered.

"For here? He's never late."

"He's leaving us for parts unknown, Pauli, going to follow his star," Stella told her.

"But I'm the star. . . or is it Star who's the star?" Pauli paused. "Is he really going away?"

"So he says," James spoke.

"I'm sorry to hear that. I've been here on the shift with him for more than two years. I've gotten kind of used to his piggy ways. We've got to give him a special sendoff."

"He has strictly forbidden me to be creatively obscene with my cookery again," James pouted. "And Isadora, the poop, has ingraciously declined the one request he did have."

Pauli looked at me, "I can imagine what that was. You didn't want to be the condemned man's last meal right?"

"Well, if he had put it that way. . . " I grinned back.

"I'll think of something to do for him. Let me mull it over," Stella said.

I answered the phone.

It Takes Two, Or More, To Tango

Isadora: Sex Information. May I help you?

Caller: Hi. My name's Don.

I: Hello, Don. You can call me Isa. What can I do for you?

C: Have you ever been in a sexual three-way?

I: Why do you ask?

C: I just want to know.

I: You called me, Don. I'm not here to talk about my sex life.

Is there something about your own you want to talk about?

C: Yes, but if you haven't done it I don't know how much help you'll be to me.

I: I have been in a three-way.

C: Well, hey Miss Priss. I can't wait to tell the newspapers.

I: Okay, okay. Now what is it you want to know.?

C: Actually, I want to know what to do. I've never done anything like this before. I guess I'm nervous.

I: I guess so, otherwise, why call? Is this something you want to do?

C: Hell, yes! I think it's every man's fantasy.

I: Well, not *every* man's.

C: It's mine anyway.

I: Okay, tell me about it.

C: I've been seeing this woman, Brenda, for about a month. Last time I was at her apartment, a friend of hers, Pat, came by to borrow something. She is really a looker. After she left, Brenda told me that Pat just made up an excuse to come over. What she really wanted was to check me out.

I: Yes?

C: Well, it seems Brenda and Pat had been talking about getting it on with a man, together, you know. Brenda suggested me, and Pat said she had to meet me first. Brenda called me today at work and said her friend thought I was cute, and did I want to get together with them both tonight.

I: And you do.

C: She called me at 10:30 this morning and I haven't been able to think of anything else all day. I mean I had to go to the bathroom twice already to jerk off. I'm sorry. Did I offend you?

I: No. I know that people jerk off, even at work; maybe especially there.

C: I'm meeting them at Brenda's tonight and I don't know what I'm going to do.

I: Well, what do you fantasize?

C: Jeez, don't get me started on that!

I: What I mean is, you must have some pictures in your mind about the way you want it to go tonight, what you especially want to happen.

C: I sure do.

I: And I'm sure the women do also. After all, these are two friends who discussed it even before you came into the scene. Each of them must have some fantasies of her own.

C: Boy, I hope so. But then, what if I can't live up to their expectations? I mean, I'm not Superman.

I: Have you and Brenda had sex together before?

C: Sure, a lot. She's really hot.

I: Has she done or suggested anything when the two of you are together that you won't or can't do?

C: No.

I: Have Brenda and Pat done this before, do you know?

C: I don't know. I don't think so.

I: Have they been sexual with each other?

C: I'm sure they haven't. They're both straight. No, I think this is new to them too, a crazy idea they cooked up to try, you know.

I: Well then, you're all in this together, so to speak. But let them know what you might want or not want if there is something specific you're thinking about. Then they can do the same if there's something particular they want.

C: Hot damn, this is so exciting!

I: Far be it from me to dampen your enthusiasm, but think for a minute. How will you feel, say, if the women do get it on and leave you out? Or, how might Brenda feel if you and Pat make a hot connection together? What will that do to your relationship with her, or her friendship with Pat? Playing with sex is a tricky business. Feelings are involved no matter how lightly you enter into the thing. You might want to talk some of this over with Brenda alone before you get into it, especially if you want to be sure that it doesn't have an unwanted effect on your relationship with her.

C: When will I have time? It's going to go down tonight.

I: I'm just bringing it up for your consideration. Maybe you could just feel the situation out tonight, talk it over, and get down to it another night.

C: No way. I'm a firm believer in when-you're-hot-you're-hot.

I: Okay. What is it you want from me then, Don?

C: Just what we're doing, I guess. I wanted to think about this out loud, talk about some of my fears.

I: Okay, good. You did say you're not Superman. Are you concerned about being able to satisfy two women?

C: I was. Now that we talk about it, I feel better. I haven't always had a perpetual bone with Brenda and it hasn't seemed to matter. She almost always gets off by me using my hand anyway.

I: Okay. Look, the very least I can say about being in a three-way is that it generates creativity. There are more body parts to be creative with—three mouths, six hands. The possibilities are almost unlimited. Enjoy. Do you have anything else you want to ask?

C: No, I guess not.

I: Well I do. Would you mind calling me back and telling me how it went? I'd love to hear.

C: Would you really?

I: Sure. I don't watch soap operas on TV. This is better

C: You've got it.

I: Good luck tonight. I hope it lives up to your expectations.

C: If not, I've had a great day of fantasies, I tell you.

I: That's the spirit.

I turned around, smiling, when the call was concluded, wanting to share a happy discussion for a change. Everyone else was on the phone. I kicked off my shoes, lit a cigarette, and leaned back to listen to the babble surrounding me.

—"There are at least three party houses that I know of in your area. They're safe places if you just want to watch. Sure, disease is a risk. So is life."

—"Fucking is something you do *with* somebody, not to them."

—"You slip the condom over the erect penis, or have your partner do it, unrolling it as you go. Make sure you leave a little bit of empty space at the tip to catch the semen. It shouldn't fit too tightly. And don't forget, when you withdraw, hold on to it at the base of the penis so it can't slip off inside her."

—"Come on. If you're just going to fool around, I'm going to hang up. Do you have a serious question or not?"

James finished a call. I opened my mouth to say something to him when the phone rang again. He shrugged and punched the next button.

Doing What Comes Naturally

James: Sex Information. How can I help you?

Caller: I don't know if I can talk to a man about this.

J: Try me.

C: I can't seem to get pregnant.

J: I take it you've been doing the conventional thing to make it happen?

C: The conventional thing?

J: You have been having intercourse with a man.

C: To put it bluntly, my husband and I have been fucking like bunnies.

J: For how long?

C: We've been married for two years. I went off the pill three months ago. I thought I'd get pregnant right away. My doctor put the fear of God into me about taking my pills regularly. He implied that if I missed one and breathed wrong, I'd get pregnant in a minute. It's been three months now and nothing. My husband has a child by a previous marriage so I know there's nothing wrong with him. I'm really getting worried.

J: How old are you?

C: Thirty-one.

J: Are you in good health?

C: Very. I even had a test for sickle cell anemia before going off the pill.

J: How long have you used the pill as your birth control method?

C: For almost ten years. I'm healthy, as I said. I'm not overweight. I don't smoke. I'm aware of the risks but I felt in my case they were worth taking. No one ever said that taking the pill might screw up my fertility. In fact, that's the main reason I never tried an IUD. I've heard horror stories about punctured uteruses. I really want a baby.

J: All right, let's start somewhere. You are in good health and so is your husband. You say you fuck like bunnies, but there is such a thing as too much of a good thing.

C: Not of sex, surely?

J: Well, if you want to get pregnant . . . It takes some men time to build up their sperm count again. Fertility experts suggest that when you are trying to conceive you should limit intercourse to no more than once every 24 hours during your fertile period. And it's best for your husband not to have an ejaculaton by any method for several days before that.

C: When am I likely to be more fertile exactly?

J: I can only give you an approximate time. While you were taking the pill, you had what is called withdrawal bleeding every month, not true menstruation. In a fertile woman an egg is released from the ovary once a month, one egg usually. Sometime between the release of the egg and its trip through the Fallopian tubes to the uterus, it has to meet up with a live sperm by which it must be penetrated in order for fertilization to take place. The whole trip takes about eight days.

C: I know all that.

J: Okay. But you might not know that sperm can live inside you for up to five days.

C: I didn't know that. Hardy little fellows aren't they?

J: If the egg is fertilized it must continue on its path to the uterus and find an appropriate place to attach itself and proceed to grow. A great many events have to happen in just the right way. The actual ideal time for fertilization is probably only twenty-four hours out of every menstrual cycle. Unfortunately, most women can only tell after the fact when that ideal time was. It was almost certain to have been 14 days before you begin your monthly bleeding.

C: It doesn't help at all to know when the time *was*. How can I tell when it *is?*

J: In your case there is probably still a residue of synthetic hormones in your system from all those years on the pill. It might take as long as a year to re-establish your natural cycle.

C: Oh god.

J: There is a way to predict the time you're most fertile by a regular system of morning temperature readings. Your basal temperature dips, then rises in the twenty-four hour period of ovulation. But you may have to take morning temperature readings for many months in order to figure out your pattern. Then you might need to bring your daily charts to someone skilled in family planning to help you interpret them.

C: We would be wasting months!

J: You know, even couples who've never used birth control take six months, on the average, to conceive. So for now, I'd simply suggest following a schedule of intercourse concentrating on days eight through fifteen, say, of your cycle. Also, after intercourse try to lie still with your legs raised, perhaps resting on a wall, for about twenty minutes. Give those little sperm an assist on their journey.

C: It all sounds like such a chore—charts and graphs, don't make love now, you must make love then. And then to lie there like some disabled bug with my legs waving in the air! How come all those teenagers get pregnant the first time they climb into the back seat of a car? It can't always be this much work or there wouldn't be so much hoo-hah about birth control.

J: It doesn't have to be work. You and your husband can just enjoy yourselves and let nature take its course. Three months isn't all that much time. I'm just letting you know some ways of maximizing the efficiency of the process.

C: It still sounds like work, and it ought to be natural.

J: Okay, Nature Woman, try this. Pay attention to your body for the next few months. Some women experience little twinges in their ovaries when they are ovulating, like mini menstrual cramps. Also, the secretions that show up in your vagina change in consistency throughout your cycle. Have you noticed that there is more mucus and it's thicker right before your period?

C: I've never looked. How do you know so much about this, you, a man?

J: I bothered to learn. Also, I'm a nurse.

C: That explains it. All my husband knows is that you put it in here and nine months later a baby should pop out, like some sort of a vending machine.

J: Is he pressuring you to produce?

C: No. But he wants a baby as much as I do.

J: It's hard for me to explain what to look for in cervical mucus consistency over the phone, especially if you're not familiar with what it looks or feels like at other times. Just let me say that there is a change in the feel of it around the time of ovulation. You can look for it and learn to recognize it, as well as get to tune in on any ovulation pangs in your innards. Again, a family planning counselor or doctor can show you what to look for and how to check it out.

C: I suppose I can ask my gynecologist the next time I see him, but he's always so busy.

J: You have a right to have your questions answered. You're paying for medical care. Questions about your body and how it functions fall into that category.

C: You're right.

J: If you don't get satisfactory answers from him, call us back. We can give you the number of the Women's Needs Center or some other doctors specializing in family planning. In the meantime, take it easy and enjoy yourselves, you and your husband.

C: Yeah, and keep my legs in the air at the same time. Thanks for your help.

James walked over to Stella and Pauli's desks after he hung up. They were both taking a break with their phones off the hook. It was a very busy shift.

"This last call reminded me," he said to them, "do you know what's in the air in San Francisco that keeps women from getting pregnant?"

"Is there such a thing? I didn't hear about it," Stella looked concerned.

"It's a joke, you ding-a-ling," Pauli snorted. "No, James. What's in the air in San Francisco that keeps women from getting pregnant?"

James grinned wickedly, "Men's legs."

Pauli laughed and punched James playfully on the arm. "I wouldn't have told that joke to *you*."

Stella looked puzzled. "I don't get it. . . men's legs. . . oh, they're all fucking each other, not women."

Pauli rolled her eyes at James and smiled. Stella put her phone back on the hook and it rang immediately.

Only If The Toilet Seat Kisses You Back

Caller: Tell me about VD.

Stella: All about VD? There's all kinds. They're called STCs by some people these days, sexually transmitted conditions. That can mean anything from crabs to AIDS. Is there something special you want to know?

C: Yes. My wife gave something to me. That means she had to be fooling around, right?

S: No, it really doesn't. It depends on what the something was she gave you.

C: Hell, it has one of those long scary-sounding names. Anyway, it's in her vagina. You can't get any more sexual than that. If I didn't give it to her, and I know I haven't been fooling around, how else did it get there? She didn't have anything like that when we got married a year ago.

S: She could have. It depends what it is. Certain STCs like herpes can flare up under stress, and she could have had herpes since she was a kid, like a cold sore. Once you have it you always have it. Only sometimes it's active and sometimes it isn't.

C: No, she said some other name.

S: Gonorrhea? Women sometimes carry that without ever knowing they have it. The symptoms are easier to see in a man.

C: Oh, you mean the "clap." No, it's not gonorrhea.

S: What are her symptoms, do you know?

C: Her vagina is itchy, dry, red and kind of. . . well, smelly.

S: Well, I can't diagnose over the phone. Has she been to a doctor?

C: Yes. The doctor gave her some pills to take and said I have to take them too. I don't think she would've said anything about it if I didn't have to take them too.

S: Okay. It sounds like what she has isn't Monilia, a yeast infection. It's probably "trich."

C: Trick? Like in trick or treat? Some treat, huh?

S: Trichomonas. It's a little bug that lives in the bladder of a lot of healthy women and men. Men don't usually show any symptoms, but women can experience just what you described—itching, burning, a strong odor. Either trich or a yeast infection can flare up from taking antibiotics, birth control pills, douching. Even vigorous sexual intercourse can cause a reoccurrence. Even if you don't have any symptoms, you may still have some of those little bugs in your penis and reinfect your wife.

C: What a drag.

S: That's why both partners need to take the medicine. Your wife didn't have to catch it from anyone else. It just happens sometimes. I just thought of something else it could be—nonspecific vaginitis, an itchy burning vagina. No one's sure what causes it.

C: So whatever it is, it doesn't mean she has to have been fooling around?

S: Nope.

C: Good. Then I'll just keep my mouth shut and take my medicine.

S: It's hard to swallow a pill that way.

C: What? Oh, yeah. Thanks for the good news.

S: You're welcome.

The evening shift had started to drift in by the time Stella got off the phone. Pauli, James and I, and Chile, who was waiting for Stella, were in the office room. We were still trying to plan something appropriate for Sam's sendoff.

"Can't we arrange for one of those Strip-O-Grams where a naked person jumps out of a cake or something?" Chile suggested.

"Sam said no cake, or no obscene cake," James said. "Although whether the cake is obscene to him would depend on the gender of the person jumping out."

"I can just see Sam's face if it was some hunky guy," Pauli cracked. "That would sure be a surprise."

Ever the pragmatist, I pointed out that we couldn't have a stranger visit the Switchboard office, even in a cake, and suggested taking Sam out to dinner instead, scratch the stripper. Ever inventive, Pauli suggested we all have an orgy. Stella suggested a massage from all of us, complete with feathers, music, and ceremony.

"Oh, I know," Stella added. "Let's all go to the Broadway Hot Tubs after the shift. James, you can bring some goodies to eat, Isadora and Chile can buy some champagne, and Pauli and I will give him a massage there if he wants one. Anyone who wants to can join in."

"And *then* we can have the orgy," Pauli added with enthusiasm.

"I think that's a great idea," James said, and then frowning at Pauli, "up to a point."

"I'm game," I added, "as long as you all don't leave me alone with Sam, naked, in a room with horizontal surfaces, after we've been drinking champagne." Everyone laughed.

I looked at James' bulk in the rickety swivel chair, and wondered how large the tub was if there were going to be five of us in there with him. James was *big*. I wondered. . . and blushed when I saw Pauli looking at me and grinning. I was surprised that she didn't come right out and ask if I was thinking the same thing she was. Stella would have, if it had occurred to her to speculate on the matter. I chided myself; we should be above such sexist musings. Well, maybe not. Human is as human does, and what drew us to the sex field in the first place if it wasn't healthy curiosity? Some might call "healthy curiosity" a dirty mind. I revel in my own, whatever it is.

10

SWAN SONG FOR SAM

Sam showed up for his last Switchboard shift wearing a suit and tie. Apparently he figured that if we were going to take him out, we'd be doing it in style. He looked a bit surprised to see the rest of us dressed even more casually than usual. For James, that meant scuffed instead of polished cowboy boots.

"Well, Sam. . . " I began, and the phone rang. I made a face and spoke into the receiver.

Silver Threads Among The Gold

Isadora: Sex Information. May I help you?

Caller: I'm calling about my wife. Can you tell me, can a woman have sexual relations after the change of life?

I: Can she? Of course.

C: My wife seems to think not.

I: Has she said that?

C: She hasn't said much of anything. She's just been acting kind of. . . squirrelly the past few months. She cries a lot and won't say what's bothering her. She's packed away most of her pretty robes and nightdresses and things. Now she's talking about redoing our bedroom and getting twin beds. In a dozen ways she's acting like the physical side of our marriage is over, but she hasn't come out and said that.

I: How old is she?

C: Fifty-one.

I: Have her periods stopped?

C: I can't say for sure. She's always been a very private person. I looked through our linen closet and I don't see any more feminine stuff, pads and such, so they probably have.

I: What about her health in general? Could she be ill and not want to tell you, something like that?

C: Our doctor is an old friend. I think he would tell me if there was anything. . . serious. Maybe I should talk to him. I just don't like what's going on.

I: She's certainly old enough to be experiencing menopause. That's an extremely difficult time for some women. The body goes through so many changes, just like a second puberty. There could be emotional ups and downs, like her crying and moodiness.

C: That there are.

I: Some women experience hot flashes, tiredness, various physical symptoms that are uncomfortable or distressing. For some, the symptoms are particularly threatening to their sexual identity.

C: What do you mean?

I: Well, breast tissue sags, wrinkles appear at an alarming rate. The vagina doesn't lubricate on arousal like it once did; intercourse may become actually painful.

C: Maybe that's it.

I: For some, the fact that they can no longer have children makes them feel useless as women.

C: What can I do to help her?

I: Just talking about the changes you've noticed would be a good start. Telling your wife that you're worried about her and would like her to see a doctor, being a bit more patient of her mood swings. Some extra loving attention, compliments, back rubs, things like that never hurt anyone.

C: Okay. But what about. . .

I: There's absolutely no reason why menopause needs to mean the end of your sexual life together, and maybe she needs to hear that—from you and from her doctor.

C: If it is menopause, is there anything the doctor could give her to make it easier on her?

I: There are hormone replacement therapies, but they are controversial. Some women swear that taking hormones lets them breeze through their body changes without a qualm. It prevents weakening of the bones as well. But in some cases there are too many risks involved to consider using them. Some women may want to have tranquilizers or mood elevators available to them for the most stressful times. That's something your wife needs to discuss with her doctor, and I do hope he or she is sympathetic. What she is going through is *not* all in her head. It's a series of physical changes which affect the emotions. All you can do is show your love and support.

C: What if I can't get her to see a doctor?

I: I don't know what to tell you.

C: Would you talk to her, tell her what you told me?

I: Of course. Perhaps she would feel more comfortable speaking with a woman, especially one she doesn't know. By all means, suggest that she call us.

C: Thanks. I think I'll try that first.

Pauli took the next call.

I Want To Feel The Earth Move

Pauli: Sex Information.

Caller: I'm calling you because I want to feel the earth move.

P: What? I'm sorry. I didn't hear you.

C: I said I want to feel the earth move. I mean I want to have the kind of orgasms they write about in trashy novels.

P: What kind are you having now?

C: I'm not, or I don't think I am. I'm not sure. I figure if I can't tell whether I am or not, I'm probably not having any. Is that right?

P: Gee, I don't know. If what you expect is to have the earth move. . . little tremors maybe? Tell me some more about what does happen and when, okay?

C: When I'm with a man I really enjoy it. I like the kissing and hugging, and I love intercourse too. I get really excited. We move around a lot. Then the man comes – sometimes sooner, sometimes later. There's this explosion for him, but I just sort of gradually slide back down to where I began. There's no one specific high point for me like a man's ejaculation, except that I sort of share his, you know?

P: How do you feel then?

C: Sometimes frustrated, sometimes just worn out from all the activity, sometimes relaxed and content.

P: Do you ever masturbate?

C: Sometimes. Not very often.

P: What's that like?

C: It's very different, sort of cut and dried. I usually decide to masturbate when I'm bored or can't get to sleep. It's an intellectual decision, you know, not something I'm driven to do. I'm usually not at all turned on when I begin. I don't fantasize or look at sexy books. I just rub my clitoris.

P: Uh huh.

C: Sometimes if nothing happens after a few minutes of that, I just get bored and stop. Other times I get hot, actually warm in that area, and turned on. Then there's a sense of urgency.

P: Yup.

C: I keep on rubbing until I feel this little. . . like an electric jolt. Zap. There's a few little pulses in my clit—blip, blip. And then I feel just the way I felt before, sleepy or whatever.

P: What you just described is your standard garden variety orgasm.

C: Is it? Well, then that's the problem. It's garden variety. It's nice, but I want something bigger and more. . . important. That's so. . . measley.

P: How is it different with a partner?

C: As I said, I love all the grappling and rolling around, all that body contact. The actual intercourse is very exciting too. It feels. . . like a bigger area of pleasure. But it doesn't *go* anywhere. At least when I masturbate there is that little zap and the blips to signal the end.

P: Sounds like a rock group: Zap and the Blips.

C: Yeah. Well, you know what I mean.

P: Do you know about the sexual response cycle?

C: No.

P: Let me outline it for you quick-like so we can be using the same language. First is the excitement phase. It's just what it says, when a person first begins to get excited.

C: Uh huh.

P: There are a number of physical signs of it, but the most obvious one for a woman is the lubrication of the vagina, and maybe her breathing gets faster. Things are happening inside too, where you might not be aware of them—changes in the shape and color of the lips and inner vagina. I describe this phase as, "Sex? Hmmmm."

C: Okay.

P: The plateau phase is an increase of all this, just more excitement, really. Inside, all sorts of changes are going on, but what is most noticeable in this phase is muscular tension, especially close to your genitals—thighs quiver and your tummy and bottom tense up. I call this part, "Sex? Oh yeah!"

C: (laughter)

P: Then orgasm; now, orgasm isn't as clearly defined for some women as it is for most men.

C: I'll say!

P: It is basically the release of tension that was building up in the other phases. That release could be a series of shudders, spasms, earthquakes—if you want; or it could be a mild and pleasant "aahh." If there is an orgasm, the little blips you mentioned, the rhythmic pulsations of the clitoris and vagina are going on. But if there's a penis inside you, or you're concentrating on what's feeling good in other areas of your body, you might not be conscious of them.

C: Oh.

P. The last phase is the resolution, when your body, including the vagina, returns to its prearousal state.

C: That's the whole thing, huh.

P: In outline form. Now all these four phases are not as clearly defined as a dance routine—first two steps to the left, then wiggle, then two steps to the right, like that. It's possible to move into and out of each of these phases at varying speeds, or so quickly that you seem to miss some. There you are minding your own business, maybe reading a mystery story, and your lover comes along and lingeringly kisses your neck. You might go from a neutral pre-excitement phase to orgasm in 10 seconds, if neck kisses do it for you.

C: Don't I wish.

P: Or you've gone through orgasm, one, two, three, and the last blip hasn't even faded away when there goes the mad neck kisser again and zip, you're in phase two, plateau, and ready to come again; no resolution phase at all. Did you get all that?

C: Yes, in theory.

P: Okay, what might be happening for you in intercourse is that you might be going from plateau into resolution without having an orgasm. You might be loving the stimulation you are getting, but it isn't exactly what you need to get off. Or, you might be having an orgasm, but since it's not what you expect, you're just not recognizing it.

C: What can I do about that?

P: Well, one thing is that when you are most excited, you can get your clitoris rubbed—your partner or you yourself can do it, if that's what brings you to an orgasm you're familiar with.

C: That's too complicated. If he's inside me there doesn't seem to be room enough for a hand or fingers or whatever. Also, I'm feeling good all over my body, or all inside me, and I don't want to leave off all that good stuff to concentrate solely on one spot.

P: Yeah, I understand that. I share your feelings, as a matter of fact. I hardly ever come from intercourse.

C: You don't? What do you do then, may I ask?

P: My main man usually brings me to orgasm after we've had intercourse. He stays in me as long as he's hard, and then uses his hand or his tongue to bring me off.

C: He goes down on you after he's come inside you?

P: Yes.

C: That sounds so. . . messy.

P: Well, if so, he's the one who made the mess. I mean, all it is is his juices and mine.

C: Yes, but. . .

P: Could your partner use his hand then?

C: I guess so.

P: Well, look, you can do what you want and whatever feels comfortable. He can do you before you fuck, ball, whatever you call it, so that he can start intercourse when you're in resolution phase and bring you right back up there. He can stop fucking when you're in plateau, get you off with his hand or mouth, and then start again. He can do you afterwards if you still want to come. There is no program for this. If you're unsatisfied after the intercourse is over, if you feel frustrated, *do* something about it. Even if you have had an orgasm you might want more.

C: But if he uses his hand, it's not the same.

P: Right. The earth doesn't move.

C: Right.

P: Well, kiddo, what can I tell you? Do you know that song Peggy Lee sings, "Is That All There Is?" Your orgasms may just not be earth movers.

C: And that's it?

P: There are body workers—not like automobile repair shops, but people who do energy realignments, relaxation and breathing techniques. They say that a person can learn to experience more intense orgasms.

C: Do you believe that's true?

P: I can't say from personal experience. It might be worth exploring. Also, next time you have sex try and pay attention to what's happening in your body. Maybe you can figure out whether you're getting stuck at the plateau phase, or moving through to orgasm and resolution without recognizing it.

C: Okay.

P: If you feel relaxed and happy after sex, you might very well be having orgasms, just not earth-shakers. The proof is in the pudding. . . or something like that. How did pudding get into this?

C: I don't know. You brought it up.

P: Maybe I'm hungry. Anyway, have I been any help to you at all?

C: I'm not sure. Thanks, though, for talking with me.

Pauli hung up the phone and motioned James and me into the back office to solidify our plans. Stella was on the line confronting a masturbator. "I don't think you're being serious at all. I think you're pulling my leg."

"That's not all he's pulling, honey," Pauli whispered to us both. She caught Stella's eye and made a gesture with her finger to her ear—Pauli's all purpose remedy, tell him to stick it in his ear.

"Look," Stella said calmly, "I think you're trying to keep me on the phone so you can masturbate, and that's not what I'm here for. If I'm wrong, I apologize, but I'm going to hang up now. You can call back when you're through."

She hung up and walked with us to the back room. I shook my head in admiration at her calm detachment. Pauli usually got angry at that type of caller. James was generally sympathetic. I often got rattled, avoided a confrontation and felt uncomfortable. Stella just took care of what needed taking care of: "I will do this and I will not do that." I was sorry I couldn't ever use her services as a midwife. She would be very reassuring to have around during a birth, taking care of business. In fact, a medical team consisting of little Stella and big James seemed a fine idea in any tense situation. We went off to confer in whispers while Sam took his last phone call.

All In The Family

Sam: Sex Information.

Caller: Can I talk to you?

S: That's what I'm here for.

C: How old should a girl be for her first sex?

S: First sexual experimentation or first intercourse?

C: First time she fucks. . . er, has intercourse?

S: Call it fucking or intercourse, I still can't answer your question. There isn't any "should" in these matters. Do you have a special reason for asking?

C: My wife's daughter is fifteen, and she's been coming on to me real strong.

S: Your wife's daughter. You mean your daughter or your step-daughter?

C: She's not my daughter by blood. I married my wife when Tiffany was two.

S: And her biological father?

C: Nobody knows where he is.

S: So in effect you are the only father Tiffany has known?

C: Yeah, but we're not related. If you have sex with someone you're related to that's. . . uh, what do they call that?

S: Incest.

C: Yeah, incest. I'm not talking about that, though.

S: But you are talking about the possibility of having sexual relations with your step-daughter, right?

C: She's begging for it.

S: Tell me about it.

C: She runs around the house in these little bitty shorts or nighties, sometimes in her underwear. When I watch TV she crawls into my lap and kind of rubs against me, you know. I get a hard-on sometimes and she don't move away. She don't kiss her mom goodnight, but she's always kissing and hugging and hanging on me.

S: How do you and your wife get along? Does she have anything to say about her daughter's behavior?

C: My wife minds her business, I mind mine. We don't have too much to say to each other. But we don't fight or nothing. I guess we get along okay.

S: And your wife and daughter?

C: They fight a lot. But I guess that's natural between kids and their moms.

S: Do you see Tiffany as a kid?

C: Well, she is and she isn't.

S: When she behaves in a sexual way towards you, she isn't?

C: She sure don't act like a kid then, rubbing her titties into me, and like that.

S: She may be doing just that, you know, acting like a kid who wants some affectionate attention. Does she have a boyfriend?

C: She says guys her age are drips. She's not interested in boys.

S: Not in boys, but in men? A man like you, for instance?

C: It sure looks that way.

S: What do you want to do about it?

C: I don't know. It doesn't seem right.

S: I think you are very wise to have reservations.

C: But it wouldn't be. . . uh, incest.

S: No, not technically, but it's almost the same since you've been a father to her all these years. Anyway, it is against the law.

C: It is? Who says?

S: No matter who is making the advances, a person under 18 can not legally give consent to sexual intercourse with someone over 18 in our state. That's considered statutory rape. Even if intercourse doesn't take place, if you are sexual but don't actually have intercourse, it would be considered child molesting under the law, or contributing to the delinquency of a minor, or both.

C: Jeez, I didn't know that.

S: Setting the law aside for the moment, if you and your step-daughter were sexual together and your wife found out, how might that be?

C: Shit, who would tell her? I sure wouldn't.

S: But Tiffany might. She might get angry with you and want to cause trouble, or she might want to hurt her mother. You said they fight a lot. She might regret starting something and need to talk to someone about her situation or her feelings. Could you trust her with a secret that could get you into so much trouble with your wife or with the law?

C: I don't know. I never thought about that.

S: I think it merits some hard thinking about, don't you? Besides laws to protect young people against abuse, or their own immature impulses, there are very good reasons for incest taboos as well.

C: Oh yeah?

S: There are more tensions in many families than most people can handle comfortably. When you mix in sexual activities as well, there are bound to be really serious frictions. It sounds to me like Tiffany may be stirring the already muddy waters between you and your wife. Or, you know, she might have nothing more in mind than testing her power to attract someone sexually. Young women often do that with their fathers or whatever older man is available.

C: Really?

S: As her father, it's your duty to set limits. That's what a parent does. You don't let her shit on the kitchen floor, or eat poison. You teach her what's right and you protect her from harm. Children count on parents to do that. Even if you don't feel that having sex with her would be harmful, it wouldn't improve your family situation, would it?

C: Awww . . .

S: What feels like a sexual come-on to you might be her way of asking for attention, affection, not sex. Or she might not be sure herself what she wants from you.

C: It seems pretty clear to me.

S: Have you asked her about it, confronted her with it?

C: Now how could I do that?

S: You could say something like: "Tiffany, when you run around the house half-undressed I feel uncomfortable.

Would you please put some clothes on."

C: But I like looking at her.

S: How old are you, may I ask?

C: Thirty-eight.

S: If Tiffany stays at home for the next few years the situation may heat up, you know. Are you having sex with your wife regularly?

C: Not so much any more.

S: Do you want to do something about that?

C: Well I sure don't like going without.

S: It might be easier for you to resist being tempted by your step-daughter if you were having better relations with your wife, don't you think?

C: Prob'ly.

S: If I give you the name of some family counselors in your area, would you go? You could go as a family, you and your wife as a couple, or just you alone. There has to be a better way to handle what's going on in your family. Are you willing to talk to a counselor about your situation?

C: Yeah, I guess so.

S: Good. Where do you live?. . .

Sam slowly spelled out the names and phone numbers of two family counselors, one of whom had spoken at the Training, and the address of a nearby clinic. He talked for a moment or two more, then gently laid the phone back in its cradle and turned to find us all awaiting his pleasure.

"That's it. I'm finished. What a charming note to end with. I had hoped I would leave with one of my favorites, a jerk-off call."

"I guess I got the call meant for you, Sam," Stella said. "I took one a few minutes ago."

"If you want to stick around," I added, "I'm sure there'll

be another along shortly. They're more dependable than City buses."

"No, thank you. I've had enough. I'm ready for my surprise adventure."

"Well, we're not," said Pauli. "Let the others go on ahead. You and I can take another call or two to see if we can send you off on an up note." And to us, "We'll meet you all there."

"Where's there?" Sam asked.

"Never mind. . . It's a surprise, remember? You'll see. . . more of us, I promise," Stella laughed, and we left.

11

OFF-DUTY CONVERSATIONS

Stella had, with rare tact, booked our place in the hot tub club, not in the name of Sex Switchboard, but in her own. Our reservation for two hours was confirmed, and if we wanted to stay longer, we could. It wasn't a busy night. The man at the desk assured us that he would send our friends on back when they arrived.

The rented space consisted of a shrubbery-shrouded deck on which rested a wooden tub like a giant wine vat. There was a speaker for piped-in music, a shower head over a small tiled depression, a long bench, and some clothing hooks. A bathroom was off the lobby and towels were provided. Given the size of the towel, I would certainly have some difficulty choosing which part of my anatomy was the pertinent part to cover, if that's what I was going to use it for. If I needed to go to the bathroom, I decided, I'd just drape the towel over my head and make a run for it.

There were no dressing cubicles, no screens. Only the shrubbery provided some possibility of concealment. I suppose the assumption was that whoever shared the tub, nude, would have no embarrassment about achieving that state in his or her chosen company.

Stella deftly twisted her braids and pinned them up, pulled her tee shirt over her head and her long skirt down over her ankles. She stepped out of the pile on the floor and her sandals simultaneously, and she was (almost) as she was born, and no doubt equally as comfortable. The trade mark of a soft drink I knew as a child featured a slender wood nymph, discretely nude, kneeling on a rock and dipping a languid hand into a pool. Except for the startling flame color of her pubic thatch, Stella, testing the tub's water temperature, looked exactly like her.

I fussed with some plastic-wrapped packages in the food basket, adjusted the ice packing around the champagne bottles, and finally turned to James and ventured, "Coming from the Wild West you can't be any more used to nudity than I am coming from the Civilized East."

"But I'm a nurse," he reminded me. "I deal with bodies all the time, many of them naked." He paused while I stood there fidgeting over my admission, and then continued, ". . . None of those naked bodies are mine, however." He grinned at me in shared sympathy. Stella was padding around, oblivious both to her nudity and our state of clothedness.

"It's not being nude in company I mind, it's *getting* nude," I mused, as much to myself as to James. "Taking off one's clothing is awkward—wriggling out of this, stooping to step out of that. Unless the act is seen through the eyes of a fond and lust-befogged lover it has got to be. . . unbecoming." But then I did a mental instant replay of Stella's graceful act of shucking off layers and decided that life is definitely different if you are 25 years old and weigh 100 pounds.

"You're talking about vanity, not modesty," James remarked with apt precision.

"That's it exactly," I agreed. "So now that I've admitted my vanity I'm going to ask you to turn your back and do something necessary with the food while I squirm out of my clothes. And when you turn around you may say something trite like, 'Why Miss Jones, you're beautiful!' and I will be grateful to you forever."

"Glad to oblige, Ma'am," James assured me, and he began to unwrap glasses from the food hamper, giving them his full attention.

Stella looked up at me in the process of my undressing, and, as if discovering a second navel, said in surprise, "You wear a bra, Isadora?" Damn! In less than two minutes Stella had made me feel awkward, fat, prudish, old, and now politically incorrect! And of course I realized at that very same moment that Stella was making me feel none of those things. *I* was making me feel them. Stella was just being herself—slender, youthful, artless Stella. I hung my clothes on a hook, bra and all, and quickly climbed into the tub. In a moment James joined us, and in another few minutes Chile was there, a jug of apple juice under his arm.

I hadn't seen James undress, but I did watch Chile. Didn't *anybody* besides me wear underwear?

There was a rap at the door and we all quieted down. It opened, and Pauli led in a blindfolded Sam who twisted his head and sniffed the air as if he could see with the ends of his brittle moustache. "Damn it, woman, this better be good," he muttered.

"Oh, you're in for the time of your life, big boy," James squeaked in a falsetto.

Sam stopped in his tracks. "What the hell is this? Pauli? Can I drop this bondage get-up and find out?"

Pauli pulled off his blindfold with a "Ta Da!" flourish. Sam smoothed any possibly rumpled moustache hairs, and his blue eyes darted around the room as he oriented himself. They fixed, as if magnetized, on the four breasts bobbing at water level. How they could skim over James' bulk or the contrast of Chile's brown skin against all that pale flesh was dramatic proof of the adage, "We see what we want to see." "How nice to see all of you here," he smiled roguishly.

"Until they stand up and I drop my jeans, you haven't seen all of us," Pauli grinned and dropped her clothes where she stood. Sam turned his back, positioning himself next to a large fern, as close as he could without actually stepping into the pot, as he undressed. I could see that the line of modesty was drawn at the generation gap.

James heaved himself out of the tub and opened and poured the champagne. He carried his large body with dignity and only his feet, without their customary boots, seemed naked to me.

When we were all seated in the tub, knees bumping, Pauli raised her glass and we all did the same. "To Sam, long may he wave." Sam tilted his glass to each in the circle in acknowledgment of the toast. "I'd prefer 'Long may he stand,' but thank you for all your good wishes." We clinked, we sipped and there was silence. Stella passed around a can of cashews. I looked at us all, six diverse people sitting together in a hot tub, drinking champagne in the fading light of a late summer evening. "Sam, I hope you take this picture with you on your travels, a mental snapshot of the good life."

Sam began to warble, "Gee, how I'd give the world to see that old gang of mine," and then, nose at water level, peered down, giving the old lyrics a new twist.

"We all came to this city from somewhere else, right?" Chile looked around for confirmation as he spoke. "I guess we all know what it's like to look for a new life that meets our needs. But we all came here and you're leaving here. What do you expect to find, Sam?"

"I don't see this as a permanent leavetaking, Chile. What I want now is something *else*, and almost anything or any place that is not here will do for a while."

"I'm not fishing for compliments, but even if you won't miss wonderful me, won't you at least miss working at the Switchboard?" Pauli asked. "I deal with sex for a living and appreciate the folks in the volunteer community even more because of that. I can talk shop talk, and it's practically the only place were I *can* talk about my work without being treated like a freak or the Whore of Babylon."

"That's true, Sam," Stella spoke up. "You wouldn't believe how uptight the people at the Holistic Health Center are about sex, and they deal with birth!"

"Oh Stella," Sam sighed, "I don't want to offend you, but maybe they have their priorities right. Sex is beginning to strike me as. . . . trivial. Getting it up, getting in on, getting it in, getting it off. As the kids say: Bo-ring."

"So go work for nuclear disarmament, world peace, ending starvation," Stella said intently.

"For right now *I* am going to be my own cause. Disarming

Sam, peace for Sam, seeing that the inner Sam doesn't starve for lack of psychic nourishment."

"I'm world weary, so weary," Pauli did a fairly good impersonation of Marlene Dietrich.

"Do you think I'm wrong, Isadora?" Sam looked for an ally, the older generation. "Do you feel you can save the world by promoting a good sex life? Isn't it all self-interest disguised as altruism?"

"It is and it isn't," I hedged. I had sympathy for Sam and his personal pilgrimage and said so. "I do think it's important for a well-balanced life, to give something back to society, to help to shape it in our own vision. So I don't see devoting oneself to any cause as trivial. It could be Save the South American Water Beetle if that's how you order your priorities. I think the most important thing each of us can give to society is a healthy self who spreads joy and nourishment, rather than pain and damage, in his or her personal connections. To that end, improving oneself is paramount. . . and so is devoting time to improving personal connections, which include sexual concerns, our own and others."

"You're waffling," James accused, playing the devil's advocate. "There are absolutes. Isn't human sex more important than the existence of some obscure bug? And doesn't the very real fact that we might all be blown sky high in a nuclear 'incident' overshadow worries over an imperfect sex life?"

"Depends on whose imperfect sex life you're dealing with," Pauli drawled. "Don't you think the president is going to think twice about punching The Button that ends it all some Tuesday morning, if his wife promised him a blow job Tuesday night? I don't think you realize how important the atmosphere at the Switchboard is for well-being, Sam. It nourishes me to be around people who are sex-positive and non-judgmental. And then I go out into the world and nourish my friends and clients. It's a different world out there."

"But, my dear, it's the real world, the one in which most of us have to live most of the time. We in the sex biz, even part time, tend to get very insular. People in East Alice, Wisconsin and Reading, Pennsylvania do not have as part of their lives sitting around in a group whose age, gender, color and sexual preference is so gloriously varied, speculating on the private lives of world leaders, while checking out each other's usually-covered body parts."

"Well, too bad for them," Stella said, "Maybe they should. I think the world would be a better place for us all if they did."

I hadn't checked out anybody's usuallly-covered parts except for Stella's, and James's feet. I set about correcting that oversight in the last fading light of the evening. They all looked. . . "appropriate," as they should look. A friendly hand squeezed my leg. I covered it with my own and squeezed back. There wasn't a soul, or a body, in that tub that I did not, at the moment, feel at peace with, including my own.

Sam, his moustache damp and drooping at the edges, looked 'round at us all and, raising his glass, echoed my thoughts: "Peace, friends, and thank you."

CHAPTER
12

AUTUMN CHANGES

Labor Day Weekend came and went, bringing Fall's changes. I think that even those of us not tied to school schedules experience September as a time of new beginnings — nostalgic wishes for metaphoric clean books and brand new shoes. With Sam gone from our Thursday afternoons, Pauli was making an extra effort to come in regularly, but Fall meant more clients for her and it wasn't always possible.

Stella carried a full load of courses at the Holistic Health Learning Center so that, while she was at the Switchboard, her time not on the phones was spent with her nose in her texts or writhing around on the floor doing birthing exercises. Chile, our nominal shift supervisor, made an appearance when he could, rare and rushed and welcome. Actually, more often than not, James and I kept each other company.

"You know, James," I said to him one afternoon late in September, "it's not Sam's absence in particular, but I do miss the camaradarie of a full shift of people. You and I are constantly on the phone for three hours at a stretch. It's too much like work. If I devoted this much time to making business calls, I'd be making a bloody fortune."

"Surely your office isn't this decorative." James pointed to

Stella huffing away on the floor, and to the large posters of genitals on the wall above us.

"But you know, James," I continued, "even though I enjoy being here, I miss. . . I don't know. Like the Friday evening shift regularly gets together after working here and goes out to dinner, or dancing. It's the community feeling we had in Training that I'm nostalgic for, I suppose—that one big happy Switchboard family, talking about sex and feelings and relationships, the *important* things in life."

"Why don't you take the Training again next month then, or have you learned everything there is to know?"

"Actually, the idea never occurred to me, that's why."

"You can take it for free if you're willing to supervise a shift next time around," Stella panted from behind a desk.

"I'll think about it," I said, and answered the next phone ring.

The Man In The Wet Nightgown

Isadora: Sex Information. May I help you?

Caller: I did something today that I need to talk about.

I: I'm listening.

C: My wife wears silky nightgowns to bed.

I: Uh huh.

C: I think they're very sexy.

I: They're supposed to be. They're definitely not for warmth.

C: Um, well. . . today I came home from work early. I went into our bedroom to change my clothes and her nightgown was lying across the bed.

I: Uh huh.

C: Well, I was undressed and there it was, so I put it on.

I: Yes.

C: I, uh, looked at myself in the mirror and I didn't look that bad in it. I mean, it wasn't ridiculous.

I: Uh huh.

C: My wife and I are both tall and thin. I'm not a hairy man. I wear my hair longish, you know.

I: Ummm.

C: The thing is. . . I would have been attracted to me. I almost looked like my wife, like a tall handsome woman. I was really enjoying the feel of that sexy fabric against my naked skin, and I started imagining how it would feel to be stroked through it the way I stroke her. So I started touching myself while I stood in front of the mirror.

I: Yes.

C: And I. . . came. I got so turned on I had a fantastic orgasm.

I: Uh huh.

C: Well, what I want to know is. . . could I be a. . . transvestite?

I: I don't know.

C: If you don't know, who would?

I: You want an expert opinion?

C: Yes, that's why I called you people.

I: But you want an expert opinion on *your* sexuality. Why are you asking me for *my* labels? You chose the garment to wear, you can choose your own terms.

C: I don't want to be a transvestite, that's bizarre. I'm a respectable married man.

I: Transvestism means cross-dressing, dressing in the clothing of the other sex. People do that at Halloween. The Annie Hall look from Woody Allen's movie is masculine suits, ties, and hats for women. That's cross-dressing too.

C: But this isn't like that. I had an orgasm.

I: I understand. This was extremely erotic for you, not fun or fashion.

C: Right.

I: If you began to wear men's underwear made from silky fabric, would that do it for you too?

C: I don't know. I wear cotton briefs.

I: Some men like silk or nylon underwear. They generally consider themselves sensual, luxury-lovers, nothing more. What if you used a piece of the same fabric to masturbate with? How would that be?

C: I don't know. I never tried that either.

I: What I'm getting at is what exactly the nature of the turn-on was for you, and then what you might want to do about that.

C: But I don't know.

I: Silky fabric does feel good to almost everybody against naked skin. Was it the fact that it was a nightgown, a woman's garment, that you used? Was it the fact that you were wearing it that was so exciting? Was it the fantasy of being a woman and having a man make love to you? Or do you want to make love with a man, in fact?

C: I don't think so. . . I don't know the answers to any of that.

I: I'm not asking you for answers. I'm giving you food for thought – suggesting ways you might understand this experience.

C: But could I be a transvestite?

I: Let me give you an analogy: Little kids often stick a bean or a crayon or something up their nose. "Why the hell did you do that?" their parents ask. The gist of the answer might be, "It seemed like an interesting experiment." Later, the same kid might find that putting a finger up his nose feels good too. Then the kid has to learn all the social rules about when it's not okay to pick your nose, and decide for himself whether it's worth the hassle of constantly being told to get his finger out of his nose. He might decide to indulge only in private and become a closet nose-picker, or forget about it entirely until the next bright idea comes to him—like maybe cutting off his eye lashes.

C: Hell, I don't know. Nose picking!

I: You did one thing once that felt good and then you felt uncomfortable afterwards.

C: Yes.

I: Okay, now what? Do you want to experiment again with your wife, or without her but with her clothes? You can decide how or if you want to take this any further.

C: Uh.

I: If it's any comfort to you, most men who define themselves as transvestites or cross-dressers are heterosexual, and often they are married. It's much easier to have access to a wardrobe that way, if nothing else, or to have a playmate who will keep your secret, if that's what you want.

C: I guess I'm going to have to think about this. It's nice to know that. . . well, that I'm not the only one.

I: There's even a club in this city for cross-dressers, a social group which meets regularly. The men, often with their mates, get together to discuss where to buy clothing without embarrassment and other topics of mutual interest. You definitely are not alone. Just how much of a part of your life you need or want to make it is up to you. This can be an isolated incident, an area of exploration, or a whole subculture if you choose.

C: There's actually a club for people who do this regularly?

I: Yes, and books and articles galore on the subject.

C: Can I call you back and find out more about those if I want to?

I: Sure.

C: I haven't decided whether or not I want to talk about this with my wife yet, but if I don't get her nightgown to the laundromat before she comes home, I won't have any choice but to tell her. Thanks for talking to me.

I: Any time.

"He's going to get some odd looks washing dainties in the laundromat," I said to James after telling him about the call.

"In this city?" James raised an eyebrow. "I doubt it."Stella stared thoughtfully into space. "Think of the goodies for his wife if he does get into it," she mused. "Marry a t.v. and double your wardrobe."

"Words for today," James intoned.

Pauli rushed in, and still in her coat, picked up a ringing phone.

Not So Good Vibrations

Pauli: Sex Information.

Caller: Can a vibrator replace a man?

P: Can a vibrator replace a man? Where? On the job? In bed? In a person's affections?

C: You know, I mean if my girlfriend gets used to a vibrator will she have any use for me?

P: Is there anything else you do for her besides give her orgasms and relax sore muscles?

C: Sure, but. . .

P: I think I understand what you're asking. I was just having fun. Your friend just started using a vibrator?

C: One of the women in her women's group gave it to her as a present. That really pissed me off. What did she say to the other women to make them think she needed one?

P: You feel that her using a vibrator implies you're not doing a good job?

C: Yes, in bed.

P: What does she say about it?

C: She says that what's said in her women's group is private and she won't discuss it with me.

P: I can understand that. But did you tell her how you feel about her vibrator?

C: She says it has nothing to do with me. She says I have my private film collection, she has her vibrator.

P: Your private film collection, I take it, is pornographic?

C: Yes, but there's nothing wrong with that.

P: I wasn't suggesting that there is. Will you tell me how you use these films? Do you and your girlfriend watch them together?

C: Sometimes.

P: When you watch them alone, do you masturbate?

C: Do we have to go into this? What I called about is what *she's* doing.

P: I understand. I'm just trying to draw an analogy for you. *If* you masturbate with your movie collection, does it take away the interest you have in getting it on with your girlfriend?

C: No. They're two different things.

P: So are a vibrator and a man. Masturbation and partnered sex can both be part of a person's sexual expression. If she uses a vibrator when she's alone and you use your films and your hand, what difference? You said you watch the films together sometimes. You could also use the vibrator together sometimes too, you know.

C: Sure, but. . . couldn't she get. . . like hooked on it?

P: Yes, that's possible, but not very likely. Often the strongest orgasm a person can have is by his or her own hand, with or without a vibrator. There's instant feedback—higher, lower, slower, faster. But that's not all sex is about. There's kissing and cuddling. . . all the rest of that good stuff. If you and your girlfriend have a good thing going, I can't imagine her replacing you with an electrical appliance, can you?

C: I guess not.

P: I'd like to suggest you talk to her about your feelings, not in an accusing way. Instead of asking her why she's doing it, make some "I statements" about the way you feel when she does. Her reassurances about what you mean to her will be much more meaningful to you than mine. Ask her what the difference is between sex with you and sex with a vibrator. I'm almost positive you'll win the majority of the points if you're keeping score.

C: But what if I don't?

P: If you don't, then maybe you need to hear what she has to say even more. If there is something she's not getting from your lovemaking together, there might be something you two can do about it. That discussion could be a lot more constructive to your relationship than, "You go in there with your toys and I'll stay in here with mine."

C: I guess you're right.

P: After you've talked with her, if you still have some concerns you want to talk to us about, we're always here.

C: Okay, thanks.

Pauli took off her coat, opened a can of diet soda, and smiled around the room. "How are you all doing? Sorry I'm late. It's a wonder I got here at all. Busy busy."

"Working your ass off, to use the vernacular?" James teased.

"Don't I wish." Pauli patted her rounded flank. "Stella, if you keep grunting like that, you're either going to shit on the floor or have a baby."

"I wish," Stella rolled her eyes.

"What's new with you, James? Hogtie your dogie yet?"

James grinned broadly. "All but branded."

"That's wonderful," I said to him. "Next thing we know *you'll* be talking about having a baby."

"It'll be in the headlines if that happens," James laughed his deep rumble.

"It may happen to you before it happens to me," Stella sighed wistfully.

"For god's sake, Stella, what would you do with a baby in your life?" Pauli asked.

"Love it to pieces. You're right, though, now isn't the time to think about it. . . but soon."

"Are you talking about you and Chile?" I couldn't believe how quickly things changed—relationships, time, us.

"Not necessarily," Stella shrugged. "I just know I want to have a kid before I'm thirty. After I finish my schooling that will be my next major project."

"It is decidedly that," I assured her, "a major project."

"You're not sorry you're a mother, are you, Isadora?"

"Me? Never. It's one of the few experiences in my life that turned out better than I expected it would. I think I was born a mother."

"And you're not using the vernacular, right?" James teased.

"How come you didn't have a bunch of kids then?" Stella asked me.

"That reminds me of a Groucho Marx story," I answered. "He was interviewing a guest on his show who had something like eighteen kids. When he asked her why, she snickered that she guessed she just loved her husband. Groucho waggled his eyebrows, flicked his ashes and leered, 'I love my cigar too, but I take it out once in a while!'"

Pauli loved that story, slapping her thigh in a fit of cackles. "James," I addressed him. "What you said before— that really is an excellent idea. No, I'm not going to have another child. I'm going to take the Training again in October, be a shift supervisor, maybe even apply to be on the Training Staff. I've been away from the counseling field too long and I want back in. Watch out, World, Earth Mother is feeling her oats."

Pauli rummaged in her purse. "Earth Mother, I got a post card from Sam this week and he sends his love."

"To me?"

"To us all. 'The search goes on,'" she read, "'Love to all of

you who continue to engage in aural sex and verbal intercourse.'"

"Sam's way with words," I thought. That would make a
good title for something.

The phone rang and Stella, exhausted by her labors on the
floor, rose to take it.

The Raising Of Cinderella's Consciousness

Stella: Sex Information.

Caller: May I speak to Sam, please.

S: Sorry, he's not here any more. Can I help?

C: Damn! I really wanted to talk to him again before he left.

S: Is this a personal call? Are you a friend of his?

C: I'd like to think I am, in a way. No, actually we had a discussion on the phone a few months ago. I sort of wanted to
give him an update.

S: Sam is in contact with one of the volunteers here. I think
she has an address for him. Would you be willing to talk to me
about it? I'll try to pass along the info if you want me to.

C: I don't know how to do this. I mean, there's no specific
message, really. When I called him I was angry and depressed
about. . . oh, men in general, I guess.

S: Yeah, I know that feeling.

C: Well, talking with Sam gave me the sense that I didn't
have to be powerless, that I might be able to change things.

S: That's great. I'm glad to hear that. I like Sam, but I can't
feature him leading the battle for women's rights.

C: He was so kind, so clear, so. . . open with me as a human
being. I have no idea how old he is or what he looks like, but,
I tell you, I had some wonderful fantasies about him after I
talked to him. It gave me hope, knowing that a man like him
was somewhere in the world.

S: I'm sure he'd really like to know that.

C: Yes, but his starring role in my bedtime fantasies is not the point of my calling. Actually, it's beside the point. I still want what I wanted when I spoke to him—a relationship with a good and caring man. But I'm not going to whine about it or pine for it. Talking with Sam was sort of a catalyst for me. I realized that I'm tired of playing Cinderella and that the Prince is not likely to come calling at my cottage door. Fantasies are okay, but reality needs some attention too.

S: Right on.

C: I wrote something in my journal about that and I wanted to share it with Sam. I called it "The Raising of Cinderella's Consciousness." Is it okay if I read some of it to you?

S: Sure, I'd love to hear it.

C: Okay, it starts out: "I still harbor Cinderella in my psyche. She sits there in the ashes of childhood fables awaiting a Prince to give her life meaning. At almost thirty she's still there, that anachronistic slut. I want her to take her broom and smash her bitchy sisters, those harpies of her imagination. I want her to go out and buy her own fucking slippers. The Prince may not come wandering in this neck of the woods. And if he should, he'll ignore the calls of Rapunzel crying pitiously for rescue in her tower. He'll step over the comatose body of Sleeping Beauty—too much trouble. Snow White? Who needs rotten apples? The forest is teeming with heroines. Do you hear that, Miriam? The princely visit has been cancelled. The Prince was delayed, waylaid, mislaid or just laid. Why would he stop at the sight of tears and ashes of old myths? He'll meet Little Red Riding Hood first, out there hawking her basket of goodies. She's a doer, that kid. Get up off your hearth and go. Glass slippers are out of fashion for a modern woman anyway."

S: Miriam, is that your name? I love it. If you want to mail that to me I'll give you the Switchboard Post Office Box and see to it that Sam gets it verbatim.

C: Oh, I don't think that's necessary. I appreciate your listening. If you do speak with Sam though, tell him a friend wishes him well.

S: Thank you. I will for sure. Hey listen. Would you be interested in doing volunteer work. . . with us? Our Fall Training Class is coming up and you might really like it.

C: I don't know. I'm kind of busy these days . . .

S: Shopping for your own glass slippers, huh? I'll see that you get some stuff in the mail about the training if you give me your address, okay? It's Miriam what . . ."

"I'm recruiting a fan of Sam's," Stella explained when she hung up.

"The world is full of them," Pauli said, "the Fans of Sam."

"I wonder if that includes his ex-wives," I asked snidely.

"We all grow and change," James added his wisdom. "How do you feel about the woman your husband married?"

"My ex hasn't remarried," I protested, surprised.

"I'm talking about you, Isadora, the person you were when you first married, however many years ago it was."

"Ouch," I winced. "You're right, James. But I'd hate to think of Sam as the finished product in the Evolution of Civilized Man."

"And are you finished evolving?" James prodded, taking on something of Sam's style as he did.

"Of course not. The quest is never ending."

"As Sam would say," Pauli put in, "May Eros bless us on our search."

The phone rang and James picked it up.

Caller: Will you tell me about women's breasts?

James: No, I'm sorry, but I will not. You'll have to find out for yourself.

He winked at me as he hung up. "Don't we all?"

ALSO FROM
DOWN THERE PRESS/YES PRESS

Books for Adults

The Playbook for Men About Sex by Joani Blank
The Playbook for Women About Sex by Joani Blank
   Sexual self awareness workbooks for men and women
   of all ages and sexual preferences

Good Vibrations: The Complete Guide to Vibrators by Joani Blank
   A lively, well-illustrated manual for women, men and
   couples who want to include vibrators in their sexual
   activities

The Sensuous Coloring Book by Patricia Waters
   An exciting coloring book for adults which celebrates the
   joy of sensuality

Men Loving Themselves: Images of Male Self-Sexuality
by Jack Morin, Ph.D.
   A magnificent photostudy on the subject of male
   masturbation

Anal Pleasure and Health by Jack Morin, Ph.D.
   Everything you ever wanted to know. . . and more, on
   this poorly understood topic

Books for Children

The Playbook for Kids About Sex by Joani Blank
   A workbook for children, which encourages them to
   express their sexual awareness through writing and
   drawing pictures. Non-judgemental and not about
   reproduction.

A Kid's First Book About Sex by Joani Blank
   A non-workbook version of *The Playbook for Kids.* For
   children as young as six.

Let's Talk About Sex And Loving by Gail Jones Sanchez and
Mary Gerbino
   Designed to be read to children, this is a unique and
   sensitive approach encouraging parent-child discussions.

ORDER FORM

Quantity	Title		Price
_____	*Aural Sex and Verbal Intercourse*	8.50	_____
_____	*The Playbook for Women About Sex*	4.00	_____
_____	*The Playbook for Men About Sex*	4.00	_____
_____	*The Sensuous Coloring Book*	4.75	_____
_____	*Men Loving Themselves*	10.50	_____
_____	*Anal Pleasure and Health*	9.50	_____
_____	*The Playbook for Kids About Sex*	4.75	_____
_____	*A Kid's First Book About Sex*	5.50	_____
_____	*Let's Talk About Sex and Loving*	6.00	_____

Please add $1.50 for the first title and 75¢ for each additional title
for postage and handling.   _____

Enclose payment in full with your order. TOTAL   _____

Name _____

Address _____

_____

Mastercard/Visa # _____ Expiration Date _____

Please contact the Publisher for quantity discounts.

Down There Press   P.O. Box 2086   Burlingame, CA 94010